Deceptive
DESSERTS

Christine McConnell

Regan Arts.
NEW YORK

Deceptive DESSERTS

A Lady's Guide to 🕷 Baking Bad!

Regan Arts.

65 Bleecker Street
New York, NY 10012

First Regan Arts hardcover edition, March 2016.

Library of Congress Control Number: 2015938344

ISBN 978-1-941393-39-0

Interior design by Laura Klynstra
Cover design by Richard Ljoenes
Cover and interior photographs by Christine McConnell

Printed in China

10 9 8 7 6 5 4 3 2 1

For my Grandma Millie
Thank you for making me feel special.

"I'm just like any modern woman trying to have it all. Loving husband, a family. It's just, I wish I had more time to seek out the dark forces and join their hellish crusade."
—MORTICIA ADAMS

Contents

The Basics

PAGE

2

Spring

PAGE

16

Summer

PAGE

106

Fall

PAGE

162

Winter

PAGE

226

Introduction

As children, we're taught that dishonesty is unacceptable. It's usually around the same time we're fed fantastical stories about fairies who snatch teeth from under our pillows, or a robust man who annually breaks and enters to drop off toys.

I believe deception in general gets a bad rap. When we are young, our parents present the world as a magical place filled with possibilities and hope. As we get older, stress and responsibility are slowly incorporated; the truth comes out, and it's easy to become disillusioned. But just because Santa Claus isn't real and it turns out Prince Charming has an online gambling problem, that shouldn't prevent you from appreciating the real magic in life: your ability to create your own fantasy—or bake it in the kitchen! This book is my opportunity to show you how to create sweet works of art that you can eat. Nearly every recipe is mixed with a little trickery and then sprinkled with some treachery.

I should start by telling one truth: four years ago, I had never baked a cake. I mean, I had made brownies and some cookies, but otherwise nothing really mind-blowing. I can clearly remember looking at pictures of cakes online and thinking, "You know what? I should take a class or something on how to do that!" Without much free time or expendable income, I started watching YouTube tutorials and reading bits here and there online and in old cookbooks. Most of my kitchen equipment I borrowed from family or bought at estate sales. I began posting anything I made online and found people to be really encouraging and supportive, motivating me to work harder.

Society makes many of us feel that there is nobility in silence and that not making a fuss over yourself is a virtue, but I've found that if you don't do it, no one else will either! I had spent most of my life quietly waiting for something magical to happen to me. That was a mistake. Life can be every bit as wonderful as you've dreamed it to be; it just takes work on your part, and quite a bit more than is advertised. So this year, if you want an incredible birthday cake, learn how to make it yourself! Or if it's deep and meaningful love you're after and you have high expectations— get a cat!

My point is that the treasures of life really are within your grasp if you're willing to negotiate and never stop improving. Everyone has something amazing to contribute, and no matter how big or small it may be, it's valuable to us all.

This book represents how I view the world. My goal is to show you that there is beauty and there is horror… and if you can embrace the former and poke fun at the latter, you will live a wonderful life!

The Basics

Before you get to baking, I should make one thing very clear up front: When it comes to dessert, my opinion is that "diet," "light," and "low-calorie" are four-letter words. Moderation is the key to everything, and the flavor of your dessert needn't suffer. So when using this book, utilize your best judgment.

Before I began any of these projects, I had a few things to master. If you can get the swing of this first batch, any of the recipes following should be a piece of cake!

White CAKE

I once followed a 150-year-old recipe for white cake and it tasted like dry, dense corn-bread. So while I'm usually a fan of the old, sometimes the new is just better. There are several white cake recipes in this book, but this is my go-to for a simple, moist, and delicious cake!

Makes one 8-inch 3-layer cake

1 cup (2 sticks) unsalted butter,
　softened, plus more for pans
½ cup vegetable shortening
2½ cups granulated sugar
5 large eggs, room temperature
3 cups all-purpose flour
1 teaspoon baking powder
1 teaspoon baking soda
2 teaspoons salt
½ cup buttermilk, room temperature
½ cup whole milk, room temperature
2 teaspoons vanilla extract

✳ Preheat oven to 375°F and place a rack in center of oven. Lightly butter three 8-inch square or round cake pans. In a stand mixer, cream together butter, shortening, and sugar at medium speed until fully combined. Add eggs one at a time, beating between each addition until mixture is very fluffy.

✳ In a separate bowl, combine flour, baking powder, baking soda, and salt. In a third bowl, whisk together the buttermilk and milk. Add flour and milk mixtures to batter, alternating in small portions. Add vanilla and beat until completely combined.

✳ Divide batter evenly among prepared baking pans. Bake on middle rack for 25 to 35 minutes, until a toothpick inserted into centers comes out clean and tops are just browned. Allow to cool on a rack for 10 minutes before removing from pans. Immediately wrap in plastic wrap and refrigerate until chilled and ready to assemble.

Chocolate
CAKE

If you're looking to tie down a man but are too lazy to feign a pregnancy, this next recipe is an easy and delicious alternative. It's pretty hard to mess up a chocolate cake, but there are some that are better than others. In my opinion, this is the best!

Makes one 8-inch 3-layer cake

Softened unsalted butter for pans

2 cups all-purpose flour, plus more
   for pans

2 cups granulated sugar

¾ cup cocoa powder

1½ teaspoons baking powder

1½ teaspoons baking soda

1½ teaspoons salt

2 large eggs, room temperature

1 cup whole milk

½ cup vegetable oil

1 tablespoon vanilla extract

1 cup boiling water

✳ Preheat oven to 350°F and place a rack in center of oven. Butter and flour three 8-inch square or round cake pans. Combine all dry ingredients in a stand mixer and blend.

✳ In a separate bowl, combine eggs, milk, oil, and vanilla. Whisk with a fork until just combined and then add to flour mixture. Beat at medium speed until smooth. Pour in boiling water and immediately beat at low speed until fully combined.

✳ Divide batter evenly among prepared baking pans. Bake on middle rack for 25 to 35 minutes, until a toothpick inserted into centers comes out clean. Allow to cool on a rack for 10 minutes before removing from pans. Immediately wrap in plastic wrap and refrigerate until chilled and ready to assemble.

Vanilla Buttercream
FROSTING

There is a time and a place for fondant (see page 11), but you should never smother your beautiful cake in it. It can be used for artistic purposes here and there, but if you care at all about the overall flavor of your cake, I strongly urge you to master the art of buttercream. It's smooth and creamy, and is more flexible to work with than you think!

Makes about 3 cups

1 cup (2 sticks) unsalted butter, softened

4 cups confectioners' sugar

1 teaspoon vanilla extract

1 teaspoon salt

1 tablespoon heavy whipping cream

✳ Cream butter in a stand mixer until smooth. Add confectioners' sugar, 1 cup at a time, until fully incorporated. Beat on medium speed until fluffy. Add vanilla, salt, and cream and whip on high speed until fully combined and fluffy.

✳ Frosting should be stored in an airtight container and refrigerated until ready for use.

Chocolate Buttercream FROSTING

This is a seriously delicious and incredibly easy recipe. I use it every time I need a smooth, rich frosting with a deep color. It complements most cakes and is easy to tint with food coloring to make darker shades.

Makes about 3 cups

1 cup (2 sticks) unsalted butter, softened
3½ cups confectioners' sugar
¾ cup cocoa powder
1 teaspoon vanilla extract
1 teaspoon almond extract
1 teaspoon salt
2 tablespoons heavy whipping cream

✳ Cream butter in a stand mixer until smooth. Add confectioners' sugar, 1 cup at a time, until fully incorporated. Add cocoa and beat on medium speed until fluffy. Add vanilla, almond extract, salt, and cream and whip on high speed until fully combined and fluffy.

✳ Frosting should be stored in an airtight container and refrigerated until ready for use.

Homemade CARAMEL

This is a recipe with a million uses! Undercook it just a bit and you'll have an incredible caramel sauce; overcook it a hair and you'll end up with a rigid glue that will hold together some of the strangest structures. My only warning is to use extreme caution when working with caramel, as it's incredibly hot and sticky. I would avoid involving children or anyone else lacking in common sense when executing this recipe.

Makes one 13 x 18-inch sheet

1 cup (2 sticks) unsalted butter, softened, plus more for pan

2 cups granulated sugar

1 cup packed light brown sugar

1 cup whole milk

1 cup heavy whipping cream

1 cup light corn syrup

1 teaspoon vanilla extract

1 teaspoon coarse salt (optional)

✳ Generously butter a 13 x 18-inch baking pan. Combine sugars, butter, milk, cream, and corn syrup in a heavy saucepan over medium-low heat and stir until sugars are dissolved. Heat slowly until mixture comes to a boil, stirring frequently. Clip a candy thermometer to inside of pot and heat and continue to stir until it registers 245°F (see Note). Immediately remove pot from heat, add vanilla, and stir vigorously.

✳ Quickly pour caramel into prepared baking pan and allow to cool. Sprinkle with coarse salt, if you like.

NOTE: For a caramel sauce, heat just to 230°F before removing from heat and adding vanilla.

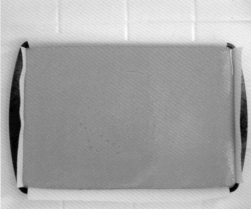

Royal ICING

Royal icing: A fancy name for an incredibly simple product. There are so many things you can do with this one, from piping and frosting cookies to using it to glue together a gingerbread house. The great thing about this icing is how forgiving it can be.

Makes about 3 cups

3 large egg whites
4 cups confectioners' sugar
1 teaspoon vanilla extract
1 teaspoon salt

✳ In a stand mixer, beat egg whites until foamy. Add confectioners' sugar 1 cup at a time until fully incorporated. Add vanilla and salt and beat until creamy. For a thicker frosting, add more confectioners' sugar. For a looser frosting, simply add water 1 tablespoon at a time until desired consistency is reached. If you go too far, you can always add more confectioners' sugar.

Modeling CHOCOLATE

I would say this is my greatest secret weapon. If you're in cake-creation mode, make a bunch of batches in lots of colors, then wrap each tightly in plastic wrap until ready to use. You can make awesome eyes for a creature by simply rolling a ball of white, piercing it with a toothpick, and dipping the back end in melted chocolate for an eyelid effect. Then simply paint or pipe on a pupil. I also use modeling chocolate for talons, tentacles, teeth, and more!

Makes about 2 cups

2 cups melting chocolate chips
   (see page 12)
2 tablespoons light corn syrup

✳ In a heavy saucepan over very low heat, melt down chips just until they reach a liquid state, stirring constantly. Remove from heat and stir in corn syrup until mixture forms a ball. Seal hot ball tightly in plastic wrap and allow to cool for at least 1 hour. After it's cooled, your chocolate can be broken off in pieces and sculpted into any shape you'd like.

Fondant

If you need something with a little more sturdiness than modeling chocolate, fondant is the way to go. And, by adding just a few drops of food coloring, you can make an endless array of colors to use. When rolling or shaping fondant, dust your surface, rolling pin, and hands with confectioners' sugar or cornstarch.

Makes about 4 cups

1 cup light corn syrup
1 cup vegetable shortening
1 teaspoon salt
½ teaspoon clear vanilla extract
2 pounds confectioners' sugar

✳ In a stand mixer, combine corn syrup, shortening, salt, and vanilla and beat until smooth. Slowly incorporate confectioners' sugar until a ball forms. Remove the ball from the bowl and knead until smooth. Wrap tightly in plastic wrap and place in an airtight container (see Note).

NOTE: Making the fondant ahead of time and allowing it to rest for a few hours can make it easier to work with. Fondant should be stored at room temperature, not refrigerated—tightly sealed, it will last up to several days.

DECORATING 101

MELTING CHOCOLATE

Also known as "candy melts," melting chocolate is a very tasty and effective decorating tool with many uses. Sold in easy-to-measure chip form in a rainbow of colors, melting chocolate has a different fat composition than regular chocolate chips and so can be easier to work with. Melting chocolate is in its most perfect liquid state at about 110°F. (If heated too quickly, though, it will seize and become useless.) If you plan ahead, the best way to melt it is in a metal pot set in an oven at the lowest possible setting, with the door open. Another method is to use a double boiler, but, in my opinion, this requires too much clean-up. A microwave is your fastest but least desirable option. If I'm in a hurry, I'll pour what I need into a heavy-bottomed saucepan and heat on low, stirring constantly, until just in a liquid state. I'll then remove it from the stove top and continue stirring until smooth and ready for use.

PIPING

There are many sizes of pastry bags and a million different piping tips that do a million different things, so when you're at the baking supply store, I suggest getting as wide a range as possible. A cake without piped edges is like a house without trim. The greatest thing about piping is that it's easy to learn how to create basic decorations, and the sky's the limit as far as how artistic you can get. You don't need an amazingly steady hand to create something very beautiful and professional!

TOOLS
Piping bags
Piping couplers
Piping tips

✳ Fill piping bags about one-third full with your icings of choice and use the desired tips to decorate as you please! Researching cakes online is a great way to get inspiration and ideas for different effects and techniques. I've learned most of what I know about piping simply by staring at pictures of other artists' work and figuring out what they did.

BUTTERCREAM ROSES

This simple technique can add a lot of beauty to your cakes and pastries. It's a little tricky to start, but after you get the hang of it, you'll see how truly easy it is!

Scissors

Copy paper

Toothpicks

Piping bag and rose tips in various sizes

Parchment-lined baking sheet or plate

✴ Start by cutting copy paper lengthwise down the middle. Then cut each piece crosswise into 2-inch-wide strips. Fold each strip in half and pierce the center with a toothpick.

✴ Fill a piping bag with fresh buttercream or very thick royal icing (for very firm roses) and pipe a small bud near the top of the toothpick while holding the end of the toothpick under the paper. Use this hand to spin the pick as you pipe. Pipe two to three layers below with the tip extending outward to create the petals. Once your rose is completed to the desired size, pull the toothpick out through the bottom and gently place your rose on the baking sheet. When your pan is filled, place uncovered in the fridge or freezer until the roses are hard to the touch.

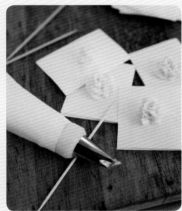

THE SCIENCE OF SCULPTING CAKES

Many of the cakes in this book are sculpted, which can be a time-consuming and somewhat complex process. But, with a few tricks, you'll be on your way to creating masterpieces!

My biggest secret to success is temperature. Everything must be as cold as possible, which can be unpleasant, but is worth the trouble when you see what you'll be able to create in arctic conditions.

I always start with cold components and take many breaks while building to allow each step to fully set while in the fridge. Because buttercream is usually the element that binds, you have to keep in mind how soft it can get at room temperature. To avoid any catastrophes in the kitchen, my advice is to crank up the AC and have plenty of patience!

THE CRUMB COAT

The "crumb coat" is a messy layer of frosting that seals in all the little bits and edges, and prevents any morsels of cake from making their way into your finished coat. Think of the crumb coat as your cake's underwear. You don't want it to show, but you need a barrier between your body and your finished outfit. It also adds stability, which is a nice bonus.

TRANSPORTING CAKES

This is, hands down, *the worst* part of the cake-making process. A few years ago, when someone was driving incredibly slowly, I used to get annoyed; now I always think, *Maybe they're just transporting a large cake in the shape of a national monument?*

I've found that a great way to transport cakes is to place a ton of freshly laundered pillows and dish towels into a sort of cushioned vortex in your passenger seat, and nestle your cake in the middle. Also, you should dress warmly, because you'll be putting your car's air-conditioning to the test—it's worth repeating that a cool temperature is your cake's best friend. And, of course, drive *very* carefully and pray to god you don't get rear-ended.

CAKE STANDS

Platters, stands, and plates are critical to the presentation of culinary artwork. I buy most of mine at yard or estate sales, but sometimes you just can't quite find what you're looking for. When I find myself in a pickle, I put on a low-cut top and head over to the hardware store. Carpentry can be tricky, but with enough planning, proper safety, and a cute outfit, you'll find it's a super-fun way to customize your own kitchenware.

HELPFUL BASIC TOOLS:
Nails
Screws
Drills
Hammer
Wood glue
Chop saw
Safety gloves and goggles
Hot-glue gun

I usually start by sketching out what I want to build, making sure it can support the weight of whatever it is I'm planning to bake. Once I have a plan and measurements, I'll head over to my local lumberyard (Rim Forest lumber has been my go-to) and collect the pieces I need.

If I want a shape I don't have a tool to create, I'll sometimes ask if it can be cut at the store. Although—fair warning—if you're asking for favors, you might want to come armed with a batch of homemade brownies.

Once you're home with your materials, the assembly, painting, and decorating is up to you!

NOTE: Always be sure to use untreated wood and nontoxic paints and glues. Keep in mind that you want to impress people, but if you accidentally poison them, the effect will be ruined.

Spring

Fruit Basket

DESSERTS

Aesthetically, you can't top the appearance of fruit. Mother Nature nailed that right out of the gate. But what if you could improve what's inside? Add some butter, copious amounts of sugar, and a lot of patience and you get something deceptively delicious and completely unique.

And what better time to bake these treats than spring? It's no mystery why it's the most beautiful time of year. The bees are buzzing, the flowers are blooming, and the smell of pies and tarts are wafting off your neighbors' windowsills. It's the perfect time of year to break out your apron and dust off your rolling pin. Make any of the following recipes and I promise you'll be the toast of any social gathering.

Caramel Apple
PIES

Makes 6 individual pies

PIE CRUST

2 cups all-purpose flour, plus more
    for molds
2 teaspoons salt
⅔ cup cold vegetable shortening
6 tablespoons cold water

ADDITIONAL
Aluminum foil
1 large apple, for mold
Nonstick cooking spray
Standard 6-cup muffin tin

✳ Mix flour and salt in a medium metal bowl. Use a pastry cutter to incorporate shortening, mixing until slightly and uniformly crumbly. Add cold water, 1 tablespoon at a time, blending as you go. Once mixture is evenly blended, quickly form into a ball. Flatten dough ball slightly with your hands, wrap in plastic wrap, and refrigerate for half an hour.

✳ In the meantime, cut six 6-inch squares of aluminum foil (heavy-duty foil works best) and form each around half of the apple to create rigid molds of the apple's shape. Lightly spray molds with cooking spray and then dust lightly with flour.

✳ Remove dough from fridge and roll out to ⅛-inch thickness. Cut out six circles roughly 6 inches in diameter. Using your hands, mold each dough circle around half of the apple as you did with the foil, to make the general shape before pressing them into your homemade foil molds. Set prepared pie crusts gently in cups of muffin tin, cover with plastic wrap, and chill in fridge until ready to fill. Wrap leftover dough in plastic wrap and refrigerate until you're ready to seal your pies.

> **NOTE:** When it comes to pie crust, keeping things cold works best. Also try to use your hands as minimally as possible.

Continued

APPLE PIE FILLING

5 Gala apples, peeled and cored
2 tablespoons lemon juice
¼ cup (½ stick) butter
½ cup granulated sugar
½ teaspoon ground cinnamon
⅛ teaspoon ground nutmeg
1 tablespoon all-purpose flour

✳ Preheat oven to 375°F. Cut apples into ⅛-inch slices or dice and toss in a bowl with lemon juice. In a medium saucepan, melt butter and sugar together over medium heat, stirring frequently. Add cinnamon, nutmeg, and flour. Cook over medium heat, stirring occasionally, until mixture is slightly thickened. Place a handful of apples in each prepared pie crust and drizzle about 2 tablespoons of the hot sugar mixture into each.

✳ Retrieve your leftover dough from fridge and roll out to ⅛-inch thickness. Cut out circles roughly 3 inches in diameter, and place one on top of each pie. Using your fingers, crimp edges to seal shut and poke several holes in centers to allow steam to escape.

✳ Still in the muffin tin, bake pies for 35 to 40 minutes, until crusts are golden brown. Allow to cool completely, then remove from foil molds and place, rounded side up, on a baking sheet lined with parchment paper or aluminum foil.

RED CARAMEL TOPPING

Homemade Caramel (page 7)
Red food coloring

✳ Make caramel as directed, adding several drops of red food coloring with the vanilla. Immediately pour caramel over rounded sides of the "apples" to create a smooth caramel skin. Allow to dry completely before applying the finishing glaze.

FRUIT PIE GLAZE

3 tablespoons apple or lemon juice
½ teaspoon ground cinnamon
¼ teaspoon ground cloves

ADDITIONAL
6 twigs, washed

✳ Mix apple or lemon juice, cinnamon, and cloves in a small bowl. Using a pastry brush, baste exteriors of pies with glaze and allow 10 minutes to dry. This gives them a realistic sheen and appearance. Insert a twig into each for some added realism.

Blueberry-Lemon PIES

Makes 6 individual pies

PIE CRUST

2 cups all-purpose flour, plus more
    for molds
2 teaspoons salt
⅔ cup cold vegetable shortening
6 tablespoons cold water

ADDITIONAL
1 large lemon, for mold
Nonstick cooking spray
Standard 6-cup muffin tin

✳ Mix flour and salt in a medium metal bowl. Use a pastry cutter to incorporate shortening, mixing until slightly and uniformly crumbly. Add cold water, 1 tablespoon at a time, blending as you go. Once mixture is evenly blended, quickly form into a ball. Flatten dough ball slightly with your hands, wrap in plastic wrap, and refrigerate for half an hour.

✳ In the meantime, cut six 6-inch squares of aluminum foil (heavy-duty foil works best) and form each around half of the lemon to create rigid molds of the lemon's shape. Lightly spray molds with cooking spray and then dust lightly with flour.

✳ Remove dough from fridge and roll out to ⅛-inch thickness. Cut out six circles roughly 6 inches in diameter. Using your hands, mold each dough circle around half of the lemon as you did with the foil, to make the general shape before pressing them into your homemade foil molds. Set prepared pie crusts gently in cups of muffin tin, cover with plastic wrap, and chill in fridge until ready to fill. Wrap leftover dough in plastic wrap and refrigerate until you're ready to seal your pies.

Continued

BLUEBERRY FILLING

4 cups fresh blueberries
¾ cup granulated sugar
¼ cup cornstarch
½ teaspoon salt
½ teaspoon ground cinnamon
¼ cup (½ stick) unsalted butter
1 egg, beaten

✳ Preheat oven to 400°F. Place a large handful of blueberries in each prepared pie crust so they are just filled. In a medium bowl, whisk together sugar, cornstarch, salt, and cinnamon. Sprinkle each pie with a scant 3 tablespoons of sugar mixture. Dice butter and dab bits over exposed fruit.

✳ Retrieve your leftover dough from fridge and roll out to ⅛-inch thickness. Cut out circles, roughly 3 inches in diameter, and place one on top of each pie. Using your fingers, crimp edges to seal. Baste top of each pie with egg, then poke several holes in centers to allow steam to escape.

✳ Still in the muffin tin, bake pies for 35 to 40 minutes, until crusts are golden brown. Allow to cool completely, then remove from foil molds and place, rounded side up, on a baking sheet lined with parchment paper or aluminum foil.

LEMON GLAZE

½ cup lemon juice
3 tablespoons whole milk
1 cup confectioners' sugar
Several drops of yellow food coloring

✳ Mix lemon juice, milk, confectioners' sugar, and food coloring in a small bowl. Using a pastry brush, baste rounded sides of pies smoothly with lemon glaze. Allow to dry completely before applying the finishing glaze (below).

FRUIT PIE GLAZE

3 tablespoons lemon juice
½ teaspoon ground cinnamon
¼ teaspoon ground cloves

✳ Mix lemon juice, cinnamon, and cloves in a small bowl. Using a pastry brush, baste exteriors of pies and allow 10 minutes to dry. This gives them a realistic sheen and appearance.

Orange Cream
CAKES

Makes 12 individual cakes

¾ cup (1½ sticks) unsalted butter,
   softened,
   plus more for molds
2 cups all-purpose flour, plus more
   for molds
1½ cups granulated sugar
3 large eggs
¾ cup buttermilk
½ cup orange juice
¾ teaspoon baking powder
¾ teaspoon baking soda
½ teaspoon salt
3 tablespoons freshly grated
   orange zest

✳ Preheat oven to 375°F. Butter and flour 12 individual-size gelatin molds. In a stand mixer, cream together butter and sugar. Add eggs one at a time, mixing well between each egg; beat until light and fluffy. Add buttermilk and orange juice and blend again.

✳ In a separate bowl, combine flour, baking powder, baking soda, and salt. Slowly add dry ingredients to wet ingredients, then fold in orange zest.

✳ Fill each gelatin mold three-fourths of the way full. Set molds on a large rimmed baking sheet and bake for 25 to 35 minutes, until a toothpick inserted into centers comes out clean. Allow to cool for 10 minutes before turning out cakes onto pan. Chill cakes in refrigerator while you prepare frosting.

ORANGE BUTTERCREAM FROSTING

1 cup (2 sticks) unsalted butter,
   softened
4 cups confectioners' sugar
1 teaspoon orange extract
1 teaspoon salt
1 tablespoon whole milk
1 teaspoon vanilla extract
Several drops of orange food coloring

✳ Cream butter in a stand mixer until smooth. Slowly add confectioners' sugar, 1 cup at a time, beating until fluffy. Add orange extract, salt, milk, and vanilla. Beat until smooth. Incorporate drops of food coloring until desired shade is reached.

✳ Cover cakes with a smooth coat of orange buttercream. Chill for a few minutes until frosting is firm, and then use water-moistened fingertips to smooth surface completely. Chill again.

ORANGE GLAZE

½ cup confectioners' sugar
2 tablespoons whole milk
½ teaspoon orange extract
¼ teaspoon ground cinnamon
⅛ teaspoon ground cloves
Several drops of orange food coloring

✳ Whisk confectioners' sugar, milk, orange extract, cinnamon, cloves, and orange food coloring in a small bowl. Using a pastry brush, baste chilled and frosted cakes with the glaze until a realistic orange appearance is achieved. Using a toothpick, add small dimples to create an orange peel effect. Allow 10 minutes to dry before serving.

Banana BREAD

Makes 6 individual tea cakes

Nonstick cooking spray

1½ cups all-purpose flour, plus more for molds

3 large, very ripe bananas

⅓ cup unsalted butter, melted

1 cup granulated sugar

1 egg

2 teaspoons vanilla extract

1 teaspoon baking soda

1 teaspoon salt

✳ Preheat oven to 375°F. Wrap a sheet of heavy-duty aluminum foil lengthwise over one side of a banana. Create 6 foil molds using this method and lay them on a large rimmed baking sheet. Lightly spray molds with cooking spray and dust lightly with flour. Set aside.

✳ Peel bananas and mash in a medium bowl. Add melted butter, sugar, and egg. Beat by hand until blended. Add vanilla, baking soda, salt, and flour. Mix until just combined.

✳ Pour batter into a piping bag fitted with a large round tip. Pipe batter into your banana molds, filling each about three-fourths of the way to the top. Bake for 25 to 30 minutes, until a toothpick inserted into centers comes out clean and tops are puffy and a crisp brown.

✳ Allow to cool completely, then remove from foil molds. Chill until cold to the touch before frosting.

BANANA BUTTERCREAM FROSTING

1 cup (2 sticks) unsalted butter,
    softened
4 cups confectioners' sugar
1 teaspoon salt
1 teaspoon vanilla extract
1 teaspoon banana flavoring
Several drops yellow food coloring

✳ Cream butter in a stand mixer until smooth. Slowly incorporate confectioners' sugar, beating until fluffy. Add salt, vanilla, and banana extract. Beat until smooth. Incorporate drops of food coloring until desired shade is reached.

✳ Coat each banana bread smoothly with frosting until bread is completely concealed. Chill for a few minutes, until frosting is firm, and then use water-moistened fingertips to smooth surface completely. Chill again.

BRUISED BANANA GLAZE

1 tablespoon vodka
½ teaspoon ground cloves
1 drop of black food coloring
½ teaspoon ground cinnamon

✳ Mix vodka, cloves, food coloring, and cinnamon in a shot glass. Using a fine-point brush, do the final decorating by dotting the "bananas" randomly, painting thin strips along the edges, and using a heavy dose of the mixture on the tips, all to make them look like ripe bananas. Allow to firm up and chill in the refrigerator until ready to serve.

Pear TARTS

Makes 6 individual tarts

PIE CRUST

2 cups all-purpose flour, plus more
for molds
2 teaspoons salt
⅔ cup cold vegetable shortening
6 tablespoons cold water

ADDITIONAL
1 large pear, for mold
Nonstick cooking spray
Standard 6-cup muffin tin

✳ Mix flour and salt in a medium metal bowl. Use a pastry cutter to incorporate shortening, mixing until slightly and uniformly crumbly. Add cold water, 1 tablespoon at a time, blending as you go. Once mixture is evenly blended, quickly form into a ball. Flatten dough ball slightly with your hands, wrap in plastic wrap, and refrigerate for half an hour.

✳ In the meantime, cut six 6-inch squares of aluminum foil (heavy-duty foil works best) and form each around half of the pear to create rigid molds of the pear's shape. Lightly spray molds with cooking spray and then dust lightly with flour.

✳ Remove dough from fridge and roll out to ⅛-inch thickness. Cut out six circles roughly 6 inches in diameter. Using your hands, mold each dough circle around half of the pear as you did with the foil, to make the general shape before pressing them into your homemade foil molds. Set prepared tart crusts gently in cups of muffin tin, cover with plastic wrap, and chill in fridge until ready to fill. Wrap leftover dough in plastic wrap and refrigerate until you're ready to seal your pies.

FILLING

5 cups peeled, cored, and sliced pears
1 tablespoon lemon juice
½ cup granulated sugar
¼ cup all-purpose flour
½ teaspoon salt
1 teaspoon ground cinnamon
3 tablespoons unsalted butter

✳ Preheat oven to 425°F. In a large bowl, toss pears in lemon juice. Place a handful of pears in each tart crust, filling them just full.

✳ In a medium bowl, combine sugar, flour, salt, and cinnamon. Sprinkle about 2 tablespoons of sugar mixture into each tart. Dice butter and dab bits over exposed fruit.

✳ Retrieve leftover dough from fridge and roll out to ⅛-inch thickness. Cut out 3-inch circles and place one on top of each tart. Using your fingers, crimp edges to seal. Poke several holes in centers to allow steam to escape. Still in the muffin tin, bake for 25 to 35 minutes, until crusts are golden. Allow to cool completely, then remove from foil molds and place on a work surface, rounded side up.

VANILLA GLAZE

1 cup confectioners' sugar
¼ cup whole milk
1 teaspoon vanilla extract
Several drops of green food coloring

✳ Mix confectioners' sugar, milk, vanilla, and green food coloring in a small bowl. Using a pastry brush, baste rounded sides of tarts smoothly with pear glaze. Allow to dry completely before applying the finishing glaze (below).

FRUIT TART GLAZE

3 tablespoons pear juice
½ teaspoon ground cinnamon
¼ teaspoon ground cloves

✳ Mix pear juice, cinnamon, and cloves in a small bowl. Using a pastry brush, baste exteriors of tarts and allow 10 minutes to dry. This gives them a realistic sheen and appearance.

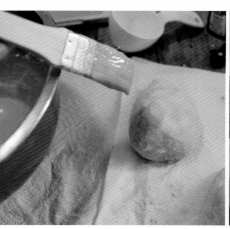

Lime
MERINGUES

Makes 15 meringues

CRUST

1 cup (2 sticks) unsalted butter,
    softened, plus more for pan
½ cup granulated sugar
2 cups all-purpose flour, plus more
    for pan

✳ Preheat oven to 350°F. In a large bowl, combine butter, sugar, and flour. Using a pastry cutter, mix until just crumbly. Transfer dough to a buttered and floured rimmed baking sheet and press in an even layer, making sure to fill the edges and corners of the pan. Bake for 10 to 15 minutes, until just starting to brown.

FILLING

4 large eggs
1½ cups granulated sugar
¼ cup all-purpose flour
Juice of 3 limes
Several drops of green food coloring

✳ In a medium bowl, mix eggs, sugar, flour, lime juice, and green food coloring until smooth. Pour over crust and return to oven. Bake for 20 minutes, until edges are beginning to brown. Remove from oven and allow to cool. Using the tip of a thin blade or knife, cut the crust into 15 lime shapes (essentially an oval with two pointed ends) and set aside.

MERINGUE

3 egg whites
½ teaspoon cream of tartar
¾ cup granulated sugar

※ Preheat oven to 200°F. In a stand mixer, beat egg whites and cream of tartar until airy and fluffy. Slowly add sugar, allowing each addition to blend completely before incorporating more. Whip until stiff and glossy peaks form.

※ Scoop meringue into a pastry bag fitted with a large round tip, and pipe onto tops of "lime" crusts to create half-dome shapes. You can use water-moistened fingertips to smooth any imperfections or distortions.

※ Place meringues on a rimmed baking sheet, about 1 inch apart, and place in oven with the door open. Dry-toast the meringues for 45 minutes to 1 hour. You'll know they're ready when they become very firm to the touch and slight cracks appear.

COLORING

Several drops green food coloring
1 tablespoon vodka

※ Mix green food coloring and vodka in a shot glass. Wait until meringues are completely dry, and then, using a pastry brush, paint until smoothly green. Allow to set until dry to the touch, about 10 minutes, before adding finishing glaze (below).

FRUIT TART GLAZE

3 tablespoons lime juice
½ teaspoon ground cinnamon
¼ teaspoon ground cloves

※ Mix lime juice, cinnamon, and cloves in a small bowl. Using a pastry brush, baste exteriors of meringues and allow to dry 10 minutes before serving. This gives them a realistic sheen and appearance.

Chocolate Yogurt GRAPES

Makes 1 bunch, or about 2 dozen candies

Several dozen yogurt-covered raisins
2 cups dark brown melting chocolate
1 cup purple melting chocolate

ADDITIONAL
Toothpicks
Waxed paper
1 Styrofoam block
1 twig, washed

✳ Insert a toothpick into the end of each yogurt-covered raisin and set aside on waxed paper.

✳ Melt both chocolates separately over very low heat, then remove from heat. Create two different shades of purple by mixing various amounts of purple chocolate into brown chocolate.

✳ Dip yogurt-covered raisins into melted chocolates several times until desired size and shade are achieved. Push opposite end of toothpicks into Styrofoam and set aside to cool and set.

✳ To create a "grape bunch," shape heavy-duty aluminum foil into a large teardrop shape resembling a full bunch of grapes. Coat top and sides of form with a thin layer of melted chocolate. Once dipped raisins have set, remove toothpicks from each grape and dip exposed edge in a bit of melted chocolate, then adhere to your foil bunch form. Repeat until you have a full bunch. Insert twig into the top as the stem, for some added realism.

Chocolate-Covered STRAWBERRIES

Makes 1 dozen

1½ cups red melting chocolate
1 dozen fresh strawberries, leaves and
    stems left on

✳ Melt chocolate over very low heat, then remove from heat. Dip strawberries in melted chocolate until skins are completely coated. Set aside on parchment paper. Heat the tip of a metal skewer and use to create small divots in the exterior of the chocolate. Set aside to cool and set.

STRAWBERRY GLAZE

3 tablespoons lime juice
½ teaspoon ground cinnamon
¼ teaspoon ground cloves

✳ Mix lime juice, cinnamon, and cloves in a small bowl. Using a pastry brush, baste the exterior of the strawberries and allow to set for 10 minutes. This gives them a realistic sheen and appearance.

✳ ASSEMBLY & PRESENTATION ✳

✳ To make a beautiful display of your creations, line a woven basket with rinsed, dry branches and leaves from a citrus tree. Gently lay your pies, tarts, breads and cakes decoratively within.

Bridezilla CAKE

It is my opinion that the majority of people are absolutely awful. Let me clarify that: I think the majority of people are capable of being absolutely awful. Not that they can't also be wonderfully nice and kind, but if given certain powers under certain circumstances, monstrous behavior can be unleashed!

Nothing sets the stage better for this than a wedding. A wedding is a magical event where you make a bunch of unrealistic lifelong promises to someone you like at that moment, surrounded by family, friends, and crippling debt.

No one is more important at a wedding than the bride. What is a bride? It's an ordinarily lovely woman who has suddenly been put in the role of dictator, with the sole responsibility of showing the world she is stylish, beautiful, and anorexic. Normally dictators have an entire country to rule over. The bride, however, is forced to choose several friends and acquaintances (by blood) to govern. These three to fifteen girls are now in charge of getting along and honoring their sovereign.

As you might guess, this is a recipe for nuclear war. Women on their own are fine, but when combined with other women, a toxic and noxious chemical is formed. This chemical reaction is especially grave for the bride. It can cause the skin to shed, revealing scales and horns, and turn normal breath into flames.

Luckily for all involved, the wedding will come and go before you know it!

Bridezilla CAKE

SHIRLEY TEMPLE CAKE

1 cup (2 sticks) unsalted butter, softened, plus more for pans

3¾ cups all-purpose flour, plus more for pans

2 cups granulated sugar

4 large eggs

4 teaspoons vanilla extract

4 teaspoons baking powder

2 teaspoons salt

1 cup whole milk

1 cup Cherry 7-Up

✳ Preheat oven to 350°F and place a rack in center of oven. Butter and flour four 6-inch round cake pans. Cream together sugar and butter in a stand mixer until fluffy. Incorporate eggs and vanilla, beating until smooth.

✳ In a separate bowl, mix flour, baking powder, and salt. Slowly incorporate dry ingredients into wet ingredients in the mixer, beating on medium speed until smooth. Add milk and 7-Up, and beat.

✳ Divide batter evenly among prepared baking pans. Bake for 30 to 40 minutes on middle rack, checking after 30 minutes, until a toothpick comes out clean when inserted into the middle of each cake; do not overbake. Allow to cool on racks for 10 minutes. Gently remove cakes from pans and let cool completely on racks before frosting.

CHERRY BUTTERCREAM FROSTING

2¼ cups (4½ sticks) unsalted butter, softened

6 cups confectioners' sugar

½ cup cherry juice

1½ teaspoons vanilla extract

1 cup diced maraschino cherries

✳ Cream butter in a stand mixer until smooth. Slowly add 3 cups confectioners' sugar, cherry juice, and vanilla. Beat on medium speed until smooth and creamy. Slowly mix in remaining confectioners' sugar and continue beating until stiff peaks form. Remove about one-third of frosting and set aside. On low speed, mix cherries into remaining frosting in mixer.

CANDY GLASS SHARDS

Softened unsalted butter for pan
3 cups granulated sugar
1 cup water
1 cup light corn syrup
1 teaspoon vanilla extract
A few drops of red food coloring

ADDITIONAL
Candy thermometer

* Thoroughly butter a large rimmed baking sheet. In a cast-iron skillet, combine sugar, water, and corn syrup. Over medium heat, stir until all sugar is dissolved; continue cooking, stirring occasionally, until mixture reaches hard-crack stage (use a candy thermometer to check; it should be 300°F). The mixture will have reduced in volume and will be producing large glossy bubbles. (Note: Stirring too much during this process will make the glass opaque, so be sure to stir only minimally.)

* Once hard-crack stage is reached, remove skillet from heat, quickly mix in vanilla and food coloring, and then pour syrup into prepared baking sheet. Allow to cool and harden completely.

* Shatter candy glass using the tip of a heavy rolling pin or a hammer with the head covered in plastic wrap.

Inexpensive 6-inch round cake pan
(a pan with 2-inch sides will give
you a little extra height and space
for the candy glass)

Drill

Three ¼-inch wooden dowels

Hot-glue gun

Modeling Chocolate, in white
(page 10)

Toothpicks

Vanilla Buttercream Frosting
(page 6)

Birthday candles (optional)

✳ For base, drill three ¼-inch holes in cake pan in a large triangle formation. Flip pan upside-down and hot-glue wooden dowels into holes to give cake additional height and stability.

✳ To shape cake into Bridezilla, trim three of the four cakes in approximately ½-inch increments; i.e., you should have one cake with a diameter of 6 inches, one that's 5½ inches, one that's 5 inches, and one that's 4½ inches. Carefully cut each cake horizontally into two layers. Place one 6-inch layer on base so dowels pierce and secure cake neatly on base. Cover with a heavy layer of cherry frosting. Place second 6-inch layer on top. Continue this process for the remaining layers, using the next smallest cake rounds for each layer. Once your structure is complete, do your crumb coat with cherry frosting.

Continued

✳ Sculpt two lizard arms and a head using white modeling chocolate. Stick a toothpick in each arm joint and at base of head. Then insert joints appropriately into cake (one arm on each side, head on top). Chill cake in refrigerator for 30 minutes.

✳ Remove cake from fridge and apply reserved cherry buttercream frosting (without diced cherries) to arms and head. Define hands and face using sculpting tools of your liking (see photo page 40). Take breaks throughout the process to chill the cake. (This process can be time-consuming, as you are actually sculpting a statue.) Smooth finished frosting coat with water-moistened fingers, then create scales on head, torso, and arms by gouging the surface with a tool of your choosing (I use a piping tip). Finish by sculpting horns, teeth, and claws out of white modeling chocolate and apply directly to head and arms (the frosting should allow the pieces to stick easily). To really give off a lizardlike appearance, I took what was left of my cherry frosting, added a few drops of red food coloring, and piped a few darker ridges all over my cake.

✳ Finish the full effect by piping on a simple wedding dress using Vanilla Buttercream. Frost the base and insert shards of candy glass all around the bottom. Add birthday candles along the edge of the base and light for a fun, terrifying effect!

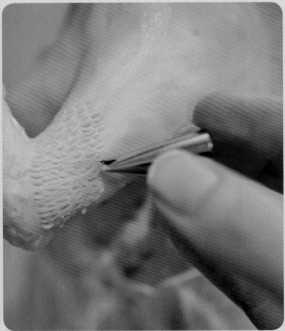

Cat Lady GELATIN

I've been a cat lady since before I knew how to spell the word "cat." There's something about feline affection that's always appealed to me. Cats are generally loving without being clingy, and they know how to have a good time, especially when an empty box is around. They're just all-around wonderful. Which is why I've never in my whole life been without one—or seven.

With anything you love, though, there are side effects. Ice cream makes you fat, shopping can break your bank, and cats can pee on your life and coat everything you own in dander. If I added up all of the time I've spent ensuring my house is clean and clear of odors and fuzz, I'd have time to live at least eight more lives!

The scene in *Christmas Vacation* where the senile grandmother brings over a cat food–laden gelatin inspired this next recipe. One thing every cat owner dreads is inadvertently sharing a treat that has caught hold of Fancy Feast, fur, or worse!

Cat Lady
GELATIN

Makes 6 servings

Vegetable oil for mold

2 cups water

4 (¼-ounce) envelopes unflavored
gelatin powder, such as Knox

Green food coloring

2 cups apple juice

1 Granny Smith apple

1 pear

1 cup heavy whipping cream

½ cup confectioners' sugar

1 cup Apple Cinnamon Cheerios

2 tablespoons ground cinnamon

White melting chocolate, melted
(optional)

✳ Lightly oil a 10-inch ring mold. In a small bowl, mix 1 cup water with gelatin and add a few drops of food coloring until desired color is reached. Let stand for 5 minutes to allow gelatin to bloom. Meanwhile, bring apple juice to a boil in a medium saucepan; reduce heat to medium. Stir in gelatin mixture and return to a boil. Remove from heat and add remaining 1 cup water. Pour into prepared gelatin mold and chill in fridge for 20 minutes.

✳ Dice up apple and pear and sprinkle evenly into gelatin. Place back in fridge and allow to set for 4 hours.

✳ Fill your sink or a large bowl with warm water and dip in exterior of mold for a few seconds. (Be careful not to let water run over top of mold.) Place a serving tray over the mold and flip the two together, gently releasing gelatin mold onto tray.

✳ In a stand mixer, beat cream and confectioners' sugar until stiff peaks form. Fill a pastry bag fitted with a large round tip with the sweetened whipped cream and pipe a spiral mound into center of gelatin. In a small bowl, mix Cheerios with cinnamon and strategically place on the gelatin. (I did a final embellishment by hand-painting kitty paw prints in melted white chocolate around the edges of the serving tray.)

Red Velvet Reptilian CAKE

Motherhood is a beautiful thing, not just for humans but for many creatures in the animal kingdom as well—and it doesn't stop there! We may have yet to reach distant planets harboring life, but that doesn't mean they aren't out there. I'm sure the special bond between a mother and her spawn extends past our solar system.

One trait that mothers seem to universally share is a desire to protect their young, and they're typically willing to sacrifice anything to achieve that—even your hand. New mothers seem especially dangerous and should be approached with extreme caution. An ill-timed movement (or comment) could cost you something that might not grow back.

My little friend here is a first-time mom from a galaxy far, far away, and while she's beautiful to look at, keeping a wary eye on her would be in your best interest. She comes from a planet made of red velvet cake, riddled with cream cheese craters and ruby-red volcanic sugar glass. As delicious as that all sounds, the surface is crawling with these protective creatures! But no worries, the following recipe will bring these critters within reach without cryo-sleep.

Red Velvet
REPTILIAN CAKE

RED VELVET CAKE

Makes 6 eggs and cake base

Softened unsalted butter for pans

2½ cups all-purpose flour, plus
    more for pans

1½ cups granulated sugar

1 teaspoon baking soda

1½ teaspoons salt

2 teaspoons cocoa powder

1½ cups vegetable oil

1 cup buttermilk

3 large eggs

3 tablespoons red food coloring,
    plus more for frosting

2 teaspoons vanilla extract

✳ Preheat oven to 350°F. Butter and flour three 6-inch round cake pans. In a stand mixer, combine flour, sugar, baking soda, salt, cocoa powder, oil, buttermilk, eggs, red food coloring, and vanilla. Beat on medium-high speed until smooth.

✳ Divide batter evenly among prepared pans and bake for about 30 minutes, until a toothpick comes out clean when inserted into the middle of each cake. Allow to cool completely on racks while you make the frosting.

CREAM CHEESE FROSTING

1 cup (2 sticks) unsalted butter,
    softened

2 (8-ounce) packages cream cheese

4 cups confectioners' sugar

½ teaspoon salt

1 teaspoon vanilla extract

✳ In a stand mixer, cream together butter and cream cheese until smooth. Add confectioners' sugar, 1 cup at a time, and beat on medium speed until fully incorporated and fluffy. Add salt and vanilla and beat for a few more seconds.

✳ Remove red velvet cakes from pans and crumble into chunks into a large bowl. Add cream cheese frosting and, using clean hands, mix well. Form 6 egg shapes using about three-fourths of the mixture. Place cake eggs in a cupcake tin and freeze until hard. Use remaining mixture to make a base on a serving dish and set aside.

ALIEN COOKIE BODY

5 tablespoons granulated sugar

¼ cup packed dark brown sugar

1 egg

¼ cup whole milk

2 tablespoons unsalted butter, melted
    and cooled

1 teaspoon vanilla extract

½ cup all-purpose flour

ADDITIONAL

5 sheets of parchment paper

Filbert brush (available at any art-
    supply store; make sure it hasn't
    been used for painting!)

✳ Preheat oven to 375°F. In a medium bowl, mix both sugars with egg until smooth. Stir in milk, melted butter, and vanilla. Add flour and whisk until light and smooth in color.

✳ On one sheet of parchment paper, draw out the general shape of your creature's body, including head and tail. On the other four sheets, draw or trace the same shape, reducing in size each time by about ½ inch around the entire outline. Using the filbert brush, paint several layers of cookie batter within the lines of your drawings to a thickness of about ¼ inch.

✳ Bake for 8 to 12 minutes, until brown around the edges. Remove promptly and bend to desired shape after cookies have cooled slightly but are still pliable. The largest layer should have the tail curled up and the opposite end curled down slightly to create the open mouth. Curve the head end up on the middle and top layers to create the open top jaw. (Using aluminum foil to make an alien body mold and laying the hot cookies on it until they firm up can simplify the process.)

SUGAR COOKIE LEGS

¾ cup (1½ sticks) butter, softened, plus
    more for pan

2½ cups all-purpose flour, plus more
    for pan

1 cup granulated sugar

2 large eggs

½ teaspoon vanilla extract

1 teaspoon salt

✳ Preheat oven to 400°F. Butter and flour a large rimmed baking sheet. In a stand mixer, cream butter and sugar together. Add eggs and vanilla and beat until smooth. Slowly add flour, 1 cup at a time, until fully incorporated. Finish by mixing in salt.

✳ Divide dough into four equal parts. With clean hands, mold each section into a set of legs, resembling an extended "M." Place legs on prepared baking sheet. Bake for 10 to 15 minutes, until just brown around the edges. Allow to cool completely.

CANDY GLASS SHARDS

Softened unsalted butter for pan
3 cups granulated sugar
1 cup water
1 cup light corn syrup
1 teaspoon vanilla extract
A few drops of red food coloring

ADDITIONAL
Candy thermometer

✳ Thoroughly butter a large rimmed baking sheet. In a cast-iron skillet, combine sugar, water, and corn syrup. Over medium heat, stir until all sugar is dissolved; continue stirring occasionally, until mixture reaches hard-crack stage (use a candy thermometer to check; it should be 300°F). The mixture will have reduced in volume and will be producing large glossy bubbles. (Note: Stirring too much during this process will make the glass opaque, so be sure to stir minimally.)

✳ Once hard-crack stage is reached, remove skillet from heat, quickly mix in vanilla and food coloring, and then pour syrup into prepared baking sheet. Allow to cool and harden completely.

✳ Shatter candy using the tip of a heavy rolling pin or a hammer with the head covered in plastic wrap.

2 cups Vanilla Buttercream Frosting
    (page 6)
Several drops of red food coloring
2 cups white melting chocolate, melted
Modeling Chocolate, in white
    (page 10)
Modeling Chocolate, in red
    (optional)

✳ Combine ½ cup Vanilla Buttercream Frosting with red food coloring to desired shade and place in a pastry bag. Seal the cake base with a layer of piped red buttercream.

✳ Glue legs and body cookie layers together using a brush dipped in melted white chocolate and allow to set until hard to the touch. Paint entire body with more melted white chocolate and place on red velvet base on serving dish. Use white modeling chocolate to form claws and teeth and place on alien. Finish by piping white buttercream scales on the entire alien.

✳ Remove eggs from freezer and roll in remaining melted white chocolate until smoothly coated—it may take two coats—and place in fridge to set.

✳ Finally, arrange eggs strategically around the alien and insert candy glass shards into the base, making sure the sharpest points are facing upward. For added fun, cut out a small section at the top of one egg and add a tail made from white modeling chocolate and piped with scales. Or, add a snakelike tongue to your alien reptile made from red modeling chocolate.

Texas Twister

FUNNEL CAKE

If a regular old twister was able to take Dorothy to Oz, I can only imagine where this one will send you! Possibly the emergency room?

In Texas, bigger is better, and heart attacks are no exception. County fairs are a popular social event in this state; and with a fair, comes the food.

Fair food is known for two things: being dangerously delicious and being devastating on your arteries. But I suppose gobbling grease once or twice a year probably never killed anyone. So if you've been in for your checkup and are in the clear, give this next recipe a go. What it lacks in nutritional value, it more than makes up for in sugary goodness!

Texas Twister
FUNNEL CAKE

Makes 1 twister (enough to hospitalize up to 5 people)

FUNNEL CAKE

2 cups whole milk

1 extra-large egg, beaten

2 teaspoons vanilla extract

2 cups all-purpose flour

1 teaspoon salt

1 teaspoon baking soda

2 tablespoons granulated sugar

¼ cup (½ stick) unsalted butter, melted

3 cups vegetable shortening

½ recipe Royal Icing (page 9)

Brown food coloring

Confectioners' sugar for dusting

Shredded wheat (optional)

Light brown sugar (optional)

ADDITIONAL

Hot-glue gun

One 13-inch wooden dowel

※ To create your cake stand, use a hot-glue gun to secure a wooden dowel vertically onto the surface on which you'll be displaying your twister. Make sure it's sturdy before stacking your funnel cake around it.

※ In a stand mixer, combine milk, egg, and vanilla and beat until smooth. In a separate bowl, mix flour, salt, baking soda, and sugar. Slowly incorporate dry ingredients into wet ingredients in the mixer, beating on low speed. Add melted butter and beat on medium speed until smooth. Set aside.

※ Melt shortening in a medium cast-iron skillet. Meanwhile, scoop batter into a piping bag fitted with a ¼-inch round tip.

※ When the melted shortening is hot (test by dropping in a small drip of batter; if it sizzles immediately, you're ready to go), quickly pipe a spiral of batter into the pan and cook until golden brown. Using tongs, transfer to paper towels to drain. Repeat this procedure to make rings and spirals of varying sizes, from 1½ inches to 8 inches in diameter, until all of the batter is used.

※ Stir a few drops of brown food coloring into a bit of royal icing. Using the icing to secure each piece, begin stacking your funnel cake layers, from smallest in diameter to widest, on the dowel. Once your twister is complete, dust with confectioners' sugar. Garnish surrounding area with brown sugar and crushed shredded wheat for a truly Texan atmosphere!

Almond Buttermilk

COBWEB CAKE

This is a cake flavor I'd bet you haven't tried. But once you do, I think you'll be hooked for life. It is soft and mellow—not too sweet, with a bit of crunch, and a haunting vanilla note you'll remember long after it's gone.

Cobwebs are typically associated with creepy, unkempt houses. Personally, I've always thought of them as works of art by long-dead, eight-legged Picassos. So what better way to make a cake eerie and beautiful than to adorn it with fragile little webs? Try practicing making your webs a bit before attempting on your actual cake—you'll get the swing of it before you know it!

Almond Buttermilk COBWEB CAKE

Makes 20 servings

BUTTERMILK CAKE

1 cup (2 sticks) unsalted butter, softened, plus more for pans

3 cups all-purpose flour, sifted, plus more for pans

½ cup vegetable shortening

2½ cups granulated sugar

5 large eggs, room temperature

2 teaspoons baking powder

2 teaspoons salt

1 cup buttermilk, room temperature

4 teaspoons vanilla extract

2 teaspoons almond extract

✳ Preheat oven to 350°F and place a rack in center of oven. Butter and flour two 8-inch and three 5-inch round cake pans. In a stand mixer, cream together butter, shortening, and sugar and beat on medium speed until fluffy. Add eggs one at a time, beating between each addition; continue beating until very fluffy.

✳ In a separate bowl, combine flour, baking powder, and salt. In a third bowl, whisk together buttermilk, vanilla, and almond extract. Add flour and buttermilk mixtures to batter on low speed, alternating in small portions, and beat until well combined. Divide batter among prepared pans.

✳ Bake on middle rack for 25 to 35 minutes, until a toothpick inserted into centers comes out clean and tops are just browned. Allow to cool on a rack for 10 minutes before removing from pans. Immediately wrap each cake in plastic wrap and promptly refrigerate until chilled. Now you can turn to your frosting.

BUTTERMILK FROSTING

1 cup (2 sticks) unsalted butter, softened

4 cups confectioners' sugar

1 tablespoon buttermilk

2 teaspoons vanilla extract

1 teaspoon salt

¼ teaspoon almond extract

Red food coloring

✳ In a stand mixer, cream butter until smooth. Slowly add confectioners' sugar, 1 cup at a time. Beat on medium-high speed until light and fluffy. Add buttermilk, vanilla, salt, and almond extract and beat until fully incorporated. Beat in food coloring to desired shade.

✳ ✳ ASSEMBLY & PRESENTATION

½ cup slivered almonds, toasted

One 10-inch dowel

Modeling Chocolate, in white
    (page 10)

Royal Icing (page 9)

Red food coloring (optional)

✳ Remove cakes from fridge and slice each in half horizontally. When creating your overall shape (see photo page 60), get creative! For mine, I started with an 8-inch layer at the bottom, spread on a layer of frosting, sprinkled with almond slivers, and topped with another 8-inch layer. I repeated this process with a third 8-inch layer and then two 5-inch layers. To create the sloped sides, I trimmed the edges using a serrated blade. At this point, spread another layer of frosting and almonds on the top and then stabilize with a wooden dowel through the center. Be sure the dowel is tall enough to accommodate your layers. Stack your final 8-inch layer and then alternate between frosting and cake layers for your remaining four 5-inch layers. Again, while creating my overall shape, I do lots of sculpting of the edges with a serrated blade. When your initial structure is formed, apply a crumb coat with buttermilk frosting and chill until firm before moving on.

✳ While your cake is chilling, get to work creating the oval medallions using modeling chocolate. Once the chocolate is warm and malleable, break into four medium-size and four smaller pieces. Using a tablespoon or other large serving spoon as a mold, press each of the four larger pieces into the spoon and set aside. Repeat the process with the smaller pieces using a teaspoon. Place the larger medallions around the lower section of your cake, spaced evenly, and the smaller medallions on the upper section. Decorate with piped royal icing dyed pink with a few drops of food coloring, if you like.

✳ To create cobwebs with royal icing, use a piping bag with small and medium round tips. To make the process easier, pipe several ropes of varying widths and lengths onto waxed paper. Once they've set completely, rest the ropes diagonally against the edges of the cake (upper and lower portions) and then pipe more webs over them as you like.

Kitten & CANNOLI

If you ask me what the single most wonderful thing in existence is, I will quickly reply KITTENS! They are somehow the furry embodiment of happiness. When I picture an afterlife, I envision only rolling fields of kittens. They are the definition of innocence, joy, and playfulness. If you find they do not affect you in the same way, I can only guess something is grievously wrong with you.

You've heard the question posed about the chicken or the egg. Well here's an even more puzzling riddle: which came first, the kitten or the cat lady? Most women are genetically designed to be nurturing, loving, and protective. Somewhere around ancient Egyptian times, cats realized this and set out to exploit it. What they created was a younger version of themselves so adorable, even the toughest women will become paralyzed with euphoria in their presence. Thus enslaving the females of the human race.

The only other thing in history to have such a potent effect on women would have to be dessert. Pastry, specifically, is the Achilles heel in most women's efforts to be Etch A Sketch thin. No one seems to have understood this better than the Italians, who I think have created the single most delicious combination of sugar, flour, and cream possible: the cannoli.

In a moment of cat scratch fever–induced delirium, I hallucinated a combination of the two greatest things on the planet. What came out of that is this recipe, my idea of heaven on earth.

Kitten CANNOLI

Makes 1 dozen

CANNOLI SHELLS

2 cups all-purpose flour, plus more
    for rolling
2 tablespoons granulated sugar
½ teaspoon salt
1 tablespoon unsalted butter, cut
    into pieces
1 egg yolk
½ cup white wine
1 egg, beaten, for egg wash

ADDITIONAL
½ gallon vegetable shortening
Deep fryer (they start at about $25
    and are worth the investment)
Cannoli mold
Canola oil for greasing
Margarita glass or other 5-inch-
    diameter glass or ring mold
Tongs

✳ Whisk together flour, sugar, and salt in a medium bowl. Work butter into flour mixture until coarse and uniformly crumbly. Stir in egg yolk and wine. Form mixture into a ball with your hands, then gently press into a disk. Wrap dough tightly in plastic wrap and refrigerate for 15 minutes.

✳ Scoop shortening into the deep fryer, and turn fryer on to medium heat. Roll out chilled dough on a floured surface *very thinly* (the thinner it is, the crisper the final product). Wrap cannoli mold several times in aluminum foil and oil lightly. Use the margarita glass as a template on rolled-out dough and cut around its edge. Wrap dough circle around mold and seal ends together with a dab of egg wash.

✳ Lightly baste exterior shell with more egg wash, and set in tray to be deep-fried. Lower tray into hot oil and fry for a few minutes, until dough is a beautiful golden brown. Using tongs, transfer to paper towels to drain. Repeat to fry remaining cannoli.

FILLING

2 cups ricotta cheese
1 cup confectioners' sugar
1 teaspoon ground cinnamon
¼ teaspoon ground nutmeg
¼ cup heavy whipping cream
½ cup mini dark chocolate chips

✳ Scoop ricotta into a fine-mesh sieve lined with a cheesecloth and let drain for about an hour. When ready, your fingertip will come away clean after touching the cheese's surface.

✳ Whisk strained ricotta in a medium bowl until creamy. Whisk in confectioners' sugar, cinnamon, and nutmeg. In a stand mixer, beat cream until stiff peaks form and then gently fold it into ricotta mixture. Stir in chocolate chips. Cover bowl with plastic wrap and refrigerate for at least an hour before you assemble your kittens.

Modeling Chocolate (page 10)
1 sheet edible rice paper
1 tablespoon unflavored gelatin powder, such as Knox
5 teaspoons water
2 cups heavy whipping cream
¼ cup confectioners' sugar
2 tablespoons cornstarch

✳ Make modeling chocolate in a few different colors. Here, I used pink for the ears and noses, white for the tails and pupils, and light and dark brown for the eyes. Mold the colors into the corresponding shapes—make sure to create a set for each of your kitties! Using kitchen shears, cut the rice paper into seventy-two whisker-like slices (six per kitten).

✳ In a small saucepan, combine gelatin and water and heat over low heat, stirring until just dissolved and hot. Set aside in a cool area. Begin beating cream on high speed in a stand mixer; pour in cooled gelatin mixture, confectioners' sugar, and cornstarch and beat until stiff peaks form.

✳ Fill a piping bag fitted with a large round tip with chilled cannoli filling and pipe into shells without allowing any filling to completely reach ends. Fill another piping bag fitted with a medium round tip with the whipped cream mixture and pipe a cat head onto one end of each cannoli. Insert eyes, nose, and ear pieces. Pipe more whipped cream mixture into other end of each cannoli and insert tails. Change piping tip to a very small round tip and gently pipe whipped-cream fur onto your kitten cannoli. Dot the eyes, insert whiskers last, and serve promptly!

Social
BUTTERFLIES

I wouldn't call myself a terribly social person. To be honest, people mostly terrify me. I've always preferred the tranquil company of nature. So what do you do when you're in the mood to entertain, but aren't necessarily in the mood for chatter? I'll tell you what I do: Put a bunch of sugary items outside, and before you know it, you'll be inundated with guests! Albeit the majority of them will be insects.

Luckily for me, the butterflies showed up first. Never ones to miss out on a party, butterflies are known for their beauty, elegance, and, apparently, their table manners. Another little-known fact about them (which I'm about to make up) is that they're as fond of white chocolate as I am. So I decided to make an entire tea set out of the stuff and serve white chocolate milk and biscuits.

If you happen to be slightly more socially adept than I am, I suggest you invite some real friends over to enjoy this whimsical treat.

White Chocolate CHINA

Makes one tea set (1 teapot, 4 teacups, 4 saucers)

1 package standard water balloons

1 package standard balloons

2 pounds white melting chocolate

Food coloring of your choice (optional)

Vegetable oil for molds

Saucers, for molds

Plastic wrap

Piping bags and tips

Fine-point brushes

Royal Icing (page 9)

✳ Blow up 4 water balloons about three-fourths of the way; these will serve as your teacup casts. The water balloons pop and peel off the chocolate easily, so it's best to use them for smaller, more fragile pieces. Then blow up one of the larger balloons to the size you'd like for your teapot.

✳ Melt white chocolate. For my tea set, I chose to color a small amount of the melted white chocolate with green food coloring for added decoration.

 NOTE: This is an extremely fun project to do with several people. While the china is amazingly delicate, know that just a touch of heat should help you mend any damaged pieces.

FOR THE PLATES

✳ Oil several saucers and wrap very tightly in plastic wrap. If using colored chocolate for details, pipe a scalloped edge along the backside rim. Allow chocolate border to fully set and harden, then pipe white chocolate onto bottoms, within the scalloped edge, using a circular pattern until completely coated. If just using white chocolate, you can either dip the bottom of the saucer on the surface of the melted chocolate, or paint the bottoms with the chocolate using a pastry brush. Once the chocolate has fully set and is hard to the touch, remove your chocolate saucers from the molds. You can embellish the front sides with piped royal icing or leave as is. Repeat as needed to make six saucers; set two aside for teapot base and lid.

FOR THE TEACUPS

✳ Dot a rimmed baking sheet lined with parchment paper with teaspoon-size dollops of white chocolate; these will serve as your cups' bases. One by one, dip your water balloons' bottoms down into pot of chocolate to the height you want your cups. Remove quickly and hold

suspended for a few moments before setting down on the bases you created. Place baking sheet (carefully) in freezer and allow chocolate to fully set, about 5 minutes. Remove from freezer and pop balloons with a pin. Carefully and slowly peel away remnants of balloons; if you allowed the chocolate to fully set, it should peel away very easily. Decorate rim and sides of teacups with piped royal icing and place each on a saucer.

⁂ To make the handles, trace your desired shape onto parchment paper and lay paper flat on a baking sheet. In preparation for your teapot, also create a shape for a larger handle and a spout. (I suggest making more than you'll need in case some break.) Using a medium round tip, pipe melted white chocolate onto your patterns. Allow the chocolate to fully set, then attach handles to cups with royal icing. (Keep in mind the handle will be purely decorative!) Set aside teapot handle and spout.

FOR THE TEAPOT

⁂ Now take up the larger balloon, and prepare yourself for some patience. Place a reserved chocolate saucer in freezer and allow to chill. Meanwhile, submerge large balloon deep into chocolate, leaving a decent opening, about 3 to 4 inches, on top. Immediately remove from chocolate and suspend by the balloon's knot in the freezer. (I did this by standing with my arm in and the freezer door open. Tedious, but effective.) Once chocolate has started to set, lower bottom of coated balloon down onto center of chilled saucer. Continue holding until it feels sturdy enough to let go. Close freezer and allow to set completely.

⁂ To create a dome for the lid (see photo page 68), use a less-inflated water balloon and dip it about ½ to 1 inch into melted chocolate. As with the teapot, hold by balloon's knot in freezer until fully set. Pop the balloon and carefully peel away from chocolate. Set aside.

⁂ Use a piping bag filled with melted white chocolate to adhere handle and spout to the teapot, and try to keep everything as cold as possible as you work. Attach remaining saucer on top for the lid and top with dome. Decorate using piped royal icing.

NOTE: Occasionally the balloons pop unexpectedly, so just know this is messy and there will be several duds.

Edible
BUTTERFLIES

2 sheets edible wafer paper
A set of edible inks
Royal Icing (page 9)
Food coloring (optional)

✳ These delicate treats are beautiful and are much easier to create than it looks! I searched for images of butterfly wings online and simply traced the wing details with edible ink by holding wafer paper over the computer screen, but feel free to get creative with it. Cut out the shapes using kitchen shears or an X-Acto knife, then fold wings slightly upwards (for variation, fold some tighter than others). Pipe bodies using royal icing, and insert wings onto the back of each body after icing, has partially (but not fully) set. Allow butterflies to fully set, then use a dab of royal icing to adhere them to their various positions.

WHITE CHOCOLATE MILK

1 cup white chocolate chips
½ cup heavy whipping cream
2 cups whole milk
2 teaspoons vanilla extract

✳ Melt chocolate chips in a large saucepan over low heat. Add cream and stir until very smooth. Add milk and vanilla and bring to a near simmer, stirring constantly. Remove from heat and pour into a pitcher. Chill overnight and shake thoroughly before serving.

Hummingbird CAKE

I'm not sure about past lives, but I'm definitely not opposed to the notion of having lived before. Sometimes something just resonates with you and you have no clue why.

For me, Southern living has always held a special charm. Something about the sun-drenched weather, floral patterns, and inviting accent just makes me think of home. And I'm from California!

If there's one thing I believe, it's that Southerners know food. So when you're passed along a recipe from someone south of the Mason-Dixon line, it's in your best interest to give it a try.

Hummingbird Cake is a classic Southern spice cake, flavored with pecans, bananas, and pineapple, and layered with cream cheese frosting. I don't think I need to say any more to get you interested, but I will mention that this is hands-down my very favorite cake. Which is why I made it for my own birthday last year!

Hummingbird CAKE

Makes 20 servings

Softened unsalted butter for pans

3 cups all-purpose flour, plus more
    for pans

1 teaspoon baking soda

2 teaspoons salt, plus more for pecans

2 cups granulated sugar

1 teaspoon ground cinnamon

3 large eggs, beaten

1 cup vegetable oil

1½ teaspoons vanilla extract

1 (8-ounce) can crushed pineapple,
    undrained

2 cups chopped bananas

1 cup chopped pecans

2 cups pecan halves

✳ Preheat oven to 350°F. Butter and flour one 10-inch, three 8-inch, and three 5-inch cake pans. In a large bowl, whisk together flour, baking soda, salt, sugar, and cinnamon. Add eggs, oil, and vanilla; whisk by hand until just combined. Fold in pineapple, bananas, and chopped pecans. Divide evenly among prepared pans.

✳ Bake for 25 to 30 minutes, until a toothpick inserted into centers comes out clean. Allow to cool on racks for 10 minutes. Remove cakes from pans and wrap in plastic wrap. Chill until ready to assemble.

✳ Preheat oven to 400°F. Spread pecan halves on a large rimmed baking sheet. Sprinkle with salt. Toast for 5 to 6 minutes, until you can smell them and they begin to visibly brown. Remove from oven and set aside to cool.

CREAM CHEESE FROSTING

½ cup (1 stick) unsalted butter,
    softened

1 (8-ounce) package cream cheese

4 cups confectioners' sugar

2 teaspoons vanilla extract

1 tablespoon heavy whipping cream

1 teaspoon salt

✳ In a stand mixer, cream together butter and cream cheese until fluffy. Add confectioners' sugar, 1 cup at a time, and beat until fully incorporated and smooth. Add vanilla, cream, and salt and beat on high speed until smooth.

ASSEMBLY & PRESENTATION

Vanilla Buttercream Frosting
(page 6)
Blue food coloring
White melting chocolate, melted
Modeling Chocolate, in white
(page 10)
Toothpicks

✳ Retrieve cakes from fridge. Slice 10-inch cake in half horizontally to create two layers. (Note: If the top of your cake is uneven, you can level it using a serrated blade.) Center one layer on a serving tray. Spread a dollop of Cream Cheese Frosting on and sprinkle with a small handful of toasted pecans. Place remaining 10-inch layer on top, but do not frost.

✳ Slice two 8-inch cakes horizontally in thirds to create six layers total. Place one 8-inch layer on top of the 10-inch (with no frosting in between). Alternate between Cream Cheese Frosting with toasted pecans and your remaining five 8-inch layers. Slice remaining 8-inch cake in half horizontally to create two layers. Layer on top of cake with frosting and pecans in between (do not frost the top of the final 8-inch layer).

✳ Slice two of your 5-inch cakes in half horizontally to create four layers total. Layer on top of cake, alternating with Cream Cheese Frosting with toasted pecans. Place remaining 5-inch cake upside down on top, so that the sides taper slightly. Use remaining Cream Cheese Frosting for your crumb coat. Chill until frosting is fully set before moving on.

✳ For this cake, I used a blue-tinted buttercream for the final exterior layer and untinted buttercream for some of the decorations. Frost with buttercream, then chill again until set. Smooth the finished frosting with water-moistened fingertips.

✳ Refer to the photograph on page 77 as a guide to decorating, but create your own flourishes as you like. Using plain buttercream and small and medium tips, pipe the bird cage structure onto your cake. Switch to a decorative tip to pipe along the edges and down the sides. Add roses as you like (see page 13).

＊ Line a baking sheet with parchment paper and draw out patterns for vertical flourishes. Using melted white chocolate, pipe along patterns and allow to fully set (placing in the freezer can speed this up!). Carefully place white chocolate flourishes onto cake before buttercream has fully set.

＊ To create the hummingbirds, sculpt white modeling chocolate. Insert a long toothpick into the beaks for easy insertion into the cake.

NOTE: To get symmetry when decorating, it's helpful to measure the circumference of the cake and mark with a toothpick the distance between each decoration. This way you end up with a uniform and balanced appearance.

Flying Saucer
COOKIES

I'm pretty sure if aliens arrived on Earth, their intentions would be fairly hostile. Not that I think that makes them bad aliens, but seriously, what could they possibly gain by coming here and trying to befriend us? If we think about this objectively, it would be in their best interest to enslave a few of us, BBQ the rest, and turn the earth into a pleasant little interstellar B and B.

In a few hundred years, we may have a bit more to offer, but as it currently stands, I doubt they'd benefit much from McDonald's or Viagra.

So what should we do if our big-eyed space neighbors show up in the sky one day soon? I say, run for the hills! Stay out of big cities and create a stockpile of prepackaged convenience store desserts and snacks to last a lifetime. It may also be in your best interest to bring a dentist along with you to your new cave dwelling; a lack of good dentistry is often overlooked in post-apocalyptic scenarios.

Hopefully this won't come to pass in our lifetime, and our beautiful blue marble continues to go unnoticed. That said, it's fun to daydream about the possible end of humanity in books, film—and now food!

Flying Saucer COOKIES

Makes 8 cookies

½ cup (1 stick) unsalted butter, softened
1 cup granulated sugar
1 extra-large egg
2 tablespoons vanilla extract
1½ cups all-purpose flour
¾ teaspoon baking powder
½ teaspoon salt

✴ Preheat oven to 375°F. Line several baking sheets with parchment paper. In a stand mixer, cream together butter and sugar. Add egg and vanilla and beat on medium-high speed until smooth. In a separate bowl, whisk together flour, baking powder, and salt. Slowly add wet ingredients to dry ingredients and mix by hand until just fully combined.

✴ Divide dough into 8 roughly equal pieces, then divide each piece into (approximately) a 2-inch round ball, two 1-inch round balls, two ½-inch round balls, one gumball-size ball, and one pea-size ball. Place the dough balls on the lined baking sheets with ample spacing, keeping in mind that each will flatten and about double in diameter. Bake for 10 to 12 minutes, until golden. Remove from oven and allow to cool completely.

Royal Icing (page 9)
Edible dusting powder, in silver and black
A few tablespoons vodka or bourbon
Red food coloring

✳ Building centered stacks, use royal icing to glue one medium-size and one small cookie onto both sides of each large cookie. Then glue a gumball-size cookie on one side and a pea-size cookie on the other side of each.

✳ Arrange 8 narrow-mouthed glasses on parchment on a work surface. Once the royal icing has fully set and all your cookies are in their UFO shapes, place one on top of each glass, gumball-size cookie up. Pour slightly watered-down royal icing over tops to create smooth spaceship tops. Let dry.

✳ Once the saucers are completely dry, about 1 hour (the icing should be hard to the touch), you can paint them. To make edible paints, mix ½ teaspoon edible dusting powder with 1 tablespoon vodka or bourbon. Pipe red lights underneath with red-tinted royal icing.

Fabergé Easter Egg CAKE

I'm not quite sure how Easter turned into one of my favorite holidays, but it has. In theme, it's the polar opposite of Halloween, which is clearly my first choice, but it still keeps things sweet!

The colors are soft and beautiful, and the children are happy and well dressed. I guess it may be because Easter reminds me of a wonderful time of year in my childhood; my Mom always arranged a huge Easter egg hunt and I'd spend hours roaming the lawn in search of brightly colored eggs.

One thing you learn as an adult is that there comes a day when you are the only one in charge of creating magic in your own life. As someone who craves a bit more magic than most, I spend most of the year dreaming up fun new ways to make the most of the holidays. This recipe combines some of the most wonderful things life has to offer: the beauty of Easter, Fabergé, and the unparalleled union of chocolate and peanut butter!

Fabergé Easter Egg CAKE

Makes 20 servings

CHOCOLATE CAKE

2 cups water

Softened unsalted butter for pans

4 cups all-purpose flour, plus more for pans

4 cups granulated sugar

1½ cups cocoa powder

1 tablespoon baking powder

1 tablespoon baking soda

1 tablespoon salt

4 large eggs

2 cups whole milk

1 cup vegetable oil

2 tablespoons vanilla extract

✳ Preheat oven to 350°F. In a saucepan over high heat, boil water. Butter and flour four 10-inch and two 8-inch round cake pans. Combine the sugar, flour, cocoa powder, baking powder, baking soda, salt, eggs, milk, oil, and vanilla in a stand mixer and beat on medium speed until smooth. Pour in boiling water and mix immediately on low speed.

✳ Divide batter among prepared baking pans and bake for 25 to 35 minutes, until a toothpick inserted into centers comes out clean. Allow to cool for 10 minutes before removing from pans. Immediately wrap in plastic wrap and refrigerate until chilled and ready to assemble.

PEANUT BUTTERCREAM

1 cup (2 sticks) unsalted butter, melted
2 cups smooth peanut butter
6 cups confectioners' sugar
1 teaspoon salt
2 teaspoons vanilla extract

✳ Cream together butter and peanut butter in a stand mixer until smooth. Add confectioners' sugar, 1 cup at a time, and beat on medium speed until stiff peaks form. Add salt and vanilla and beat until incorporated.

✳ ASSEMBLY & PRESENTATION

2 cups dry-roasted salted peanuts,
    chopped
Cake board, cut into a 10-inch circle
    (optional)
One 10-inch wooden dowel (optional)
Vanilla Buttercream Frosting
    (page 6)
Food coloring
¼ recipe white fondant (page 11)

✳ Retrieve cakes from fridge. Slice each cake horizontally into two layers. Place one 8-inch layer in a ceramic bowl. Spread a generous dollop of peanut buttercream on top and sprinkle with a small handful of chopped peanuts. Top with a second 8-inch layer. Frost with more peanut buttercream, sprinkle with peanuts, and top with a 10-inch layer of cake. Continue alternating frosting, peanuts, and remaining seven 10-inch cake layers. Finally place remaining two 8-inch layers on top, with frosting and peanuts in between. For added stability, you can place a 10-inch cake board at the halfway point and insert a wooden dowel to run through the entire height of the cake.

✳ If your cake needs a little extra shape, carefully sculpt the edges with a serrated blade. Use any remaining peanut buttercream for crumb coat, then chill until set.

✳ Once frosting is fully set, seal cake with a colored buttercream frosting in your chosen shade. Chill cake until final frosting is fully set and then smooth with water-moistened fingertips. Chill once more and then pipe the exterior details with plain white buttercream for a regal appearance (see photograph, left).

✳ The white top dome in the photo is made of a *very* thinly rolled piece of white fondant. I've stated before how much I dislike fondant, but every now and again you've got to break your own rules!

Vintage Spring Wedding CAKE

Spring is essentially the time of year that the earth starts anew. In many ways, it's a time for birth and new beginnings, which is why I think it's such a popular time for weddings.

It's interesting and moving to watch people you know and love grow up, find people who make them better, and start a life together with them. This set of cakes was made for my younger brother's childhood best friend. He went from being a tiny odd-looking pest into an awesome guy who found an even more awesome girl. So obviously I was happy to make them a cake worthy of such a beautiful union.

When it comes to wedding cakes, the surest way to please a ton of people is to give them choices (and these cakes were more than enough to feed the seventy wedding guests). Following are several flavors as unique as the people they were made for.

Nut Allergy–Sensitive
HUMMINGBIRD CAKE

Makes 30 servings

I invented this cake because the groom had a nut allergy, but a love of spice cake. By layering this typically nut-laden cake with brown sugar crumbles, I was able to retain the texture of a classic hummingbird cake without sending one of the costars of the event to the hospital during the reception.

Softened unsalted butter for pans

6 cups all-purpose flour, plus more for pans

2 teaspoons baking soda

4 teaspoons salt

4 cups granulated sugar

2 teaspoons ground cinnamon

6 large eggs, beaten

2 cups vegetable oil

1 tablespoon vanilla extract

2 (8-ounce) cans crushed pineapple, undrained

4 cups chopped bananas

✳ Preheat oven to 350°F. Butter and flour one 10-inch, four 8-inch, and one 5-inch round cake pans. In a large bowl, whisk together flour, baking soda, salt, sugar, and cinnamon. Add eggs, oil, and vanilla. Whisk by hand until just combined, then fold in pineapple and bananas.

✳ Divide batter among prepared pans. Bake for 25 to 30 minutes, until a toothpick inserted into centers comes out clean. Allow to cool on racks for 10 minutes. Remove cakes from pans and immediately wrap in plastic wrap. Refrigerate until chilled and ready to assemble.

BROWN SUGAR CRUMBLES

1 cup packed light brown sugar

1 cup all-purpose flour

¼ cup (½ stick) unsalted butter, diced

2 teaspoons salt

1 teaspoon ground cinnamon

✳ Preheat oven to 425°F. In a medium bowl, toss together brown sugar, flour, butter, salt, and cinnamon just until coarsely combined. Spread evenly on a rimmed baking sheet and toast in oven for 10 minutes, stirring once halfway through baking. Remove from oven and set aside to cool until you are ready to assemble.

CREAM CHEESE FROSTING

1 cup (2 sticks) unsalted butter, softened

2 (8-ounce) packages cream cheese

8 cups confectioners' sugar

4 teaspoons vanilla extract

2 tablespoons heavy cream

2 teaspoons salt

✳ In a stand mixer, cream together butter and cream cheese until fluffy. Add confectioners' sugar, 1 cup at a time, and beat on medium speed until stiff peaks form. Add vanilla, cream, and salt; beat at high speed until smooth and fluffy.

ASSEMBLY

Cake board, cut into a 12-inch circle

✳ Retrieve cakes from fridge. Slice each cake horizontally into two layers. Center a 10-inch layer on cake board. Spread a generous dollop of Cream Cheese Frosting on top and then sprinkle on a small handful of brown sugar crumbles. Repeat for remaining layers, building from largest to smallest. Once all layers are stacked, use a serrated blade to carve a dome shape. Use more Cream Cheese Frosting for crumb coat. Chill cake until ready to frost with final coat and decorate (see page 98).

Strawberry Cream
CAKE

STRAWBERRY CAKE

1 cup (2 sticks) unsalted butter, softened, plus more for pans

2½ cups cake flour, plus more for pans

2 cups granulated sugar

2 extra-large eggs

1 tablespoon lemon juice

2 teaspoons vanilla extract

4 tablespoons strawberry gelatin powder, such as Jell-O

½ teaspoon baking soda

¼ teaspoon salt

1 cup buttermilk

⅔ cup chopped fresh strawberries

✳ Preheat oven to 375°F. Butter and flour three 10-inch round cake pans. In a stand mixer, cream together butter and sugar. Add eggs and beat on medium-high speed until smooth. Beat in lemon juice and vanilla. In a separate bowl, whisk together flour, gelatin, baking soda, and salt. Add flour mixture and buttermilk to batter on medium speed, alternating for each addition. Fold in strawberries.

✳ Divide batter evenly among prepared pans. Bake for 35 to 45 minutes, until a toothpick inserted into centers comes out clean. Do not open oven door before the 30-minute mark. Allow to cool for 10 minutes before removing cakes from their pans. Immediately wrap in plastic wrap and refrigerate until chilled and ready to assemble.

STRAWBERRY FROSTING

1 cup fresh strawberries

1 cup (2 sticks) unsalted butter, softened

4 cups confectioners' sugar

2 tablespoons strawberry gelatin powder, such as Jell-O

1 teaspoon vanilla extract

1 teaspoon salt

✳ Remove stems from strawberries and transfer to a food processor or blender to purée. Transfer purée to a small saucepan and simmer over medium heat and cook until reduced by half, stirring frequently, about 20 minutes. In a stand mixer, cream butter, then add confectioners' sugar, 1 cup at a time, until fully incorporated. Add gelatin, vanilla, and salt and beat on medium-high speed until smooth and combined. Add strawberry reduction and blend on low speed.

ASSEMBLY

One 14-ounce package of strawberry glaze

Cake board, cut into a 12-inch circle

✳ Retrieve cakes from fridge. Slice each cake horizontally into two layers. Center first layer on cake board; spread a generous dollop of strawberry frosting on top. Pipe a large spiral of strawberry glaze on top of frosting. Repeat for remaining layers. Once all layers are stacked, use a serrated blade to carve dome shape. Use remaining strawberry frosting for coat crumb. Chill cake until ready to frost in final coat and decorate (see page 98).

Lemon Curd
CAKE

Makes 15 servings

LEMON CAKE

1 cup (2 sticks) unsalted butter,
    softened, plus more for pans
3½ cups all-purpose flour, plus more
    for pans
3 cups granulated sugar
4 extra-large eggs, room temperature
½ cup grated lemon zest
2 teaspoons vanilla extract
½ teaspoon baking powder
½ teaspoon baking soda
1 teaspoon salt
1 cup lemon juice
¾ cup buttermilk, room temperature

✳ Preheat oven to 375°F. Butter and flour three 10-inch round baking pans. In a stand mixer, cream together butter and sugar until fluffy. Add eggs and beat on medium-high speed until smooth; beat in lemon zest and vanilla. In a separate bowl, combine flour, baking soda, baking powder, and salt. In a small bowl, combine buttermilk and lemon juice.

✳ Add flour mixture and buttermilk mixture to batter on medium speed, alternating between each addition. Once smooth, divide batter among prepared pans. Bake for 35 to 45 minutes, until a toothpick inserted into centers comes out clean. Allow to cool on racks for 10 minutes. Remove cakes from pans and immediately wrap in plastic wrap. Chill until ready to assemble.

LEMON CURD

½ cup granulated sugar
⅓ cup lemon juice
½ cup grated lemon zest
⅛ teaspoon fine salt
5 large egg yolks
½ cup (1 stick) unsalted butter,
    softened

✳ In a medium saucepan, heat sugar, lemon juice, lemon zest, and salt. Stir over low heat until very hot but not quite simmering. Beat egg yolks in a heatproof bowl. Slowly pour ½ cup sugar mixture into yolks, while beating quickly to temper. Repeat twice more and then pour yolk mixture back into saucepan. Heat on low, stirring constantly until mixture sticks to the back of a wooden spoon. Remove from heat and add butter, whisking until creamy and smooth. Chill for at least 45 minutes before assembly.

ASSEMBLY

Vanilla Buttercream Frosting
    (page 6)
Cake board, cut into a 12-inch circle

✳ Retrieve lemon cakes from fridge and slice each cake horizontally into two layers. Center first layer on cake board. As you stack, alternate cake layers with a thin coat of buttercream and a thin coat of lemon curd. Once all layers are stacked, use a serrated blade to carve dome shape. Apply crumb coat with vanilla buttercream. Chill cake until ready to frost with final coat and decorate (see page 98).

Cherry Cream
CHEESECAKE

Makes 10 servings

CAKE

1 recipe White Cake (page 4), baked in
   three 8-inch round cake pans

CREAM CHEESE FROSTING

½ cup (1 stick) unsalted butter,
   softened
1 (8-ounce) package cream cheese
4 cups confectioners' sugar
2 teaspoons vanilla extract
1 tablespoon heavy whipping cream
1 teaspoon salt

✳ In a stand mixer, cream together butter and cream cheese until fluffy. Add confectioners' sugar, 1 cup at a time, beating on medium speed until fully incorporated. Add vanilla, cream, and salt; beat on medium-high speed until stiff peaks form.

GRAHAM CRACKER CRUST

2 cups finely ground graham crackers
⅓ cup granulated sugar
½ cup (1 stick) unsalted butter,
   softened
1 teaspoon ground cinnamon
¼ teaspoon ground nutmeg
¼ teaspoon ground cloves

✳ Preheat oven to 400°F. Combine all ingredients in a medium metal bowl and blend using a pastry cutter. Divide mixture evenly between two standard-size pie dishes (8 to 10 inches). Press mixture evenly into bottom of pie dishes, making sure bottom is fully covered. Bake for 5 to 7 minutes, until golden brown. Remove from oven and allow to cool to room temperature before assembly.

ASSEMBLY

1 (8-ounce) can cherry pastry filling
Cake board, cut into a 10-inch circle
½ cup ground graham crackers

✳ Retrieve white cakes from the fridge and slice each cake horizontally into two layers. Center first layer on cake board. Spread a layer of cream cheese frosting on it, followed by a piped spiral of cherry filling; sprinkle on a layer of graham cracker crumbs; stack another cake layer on top and repeat, using all the cake layers. Use remaining cream cheese frosting for crumb coat. Chill cake until ready to frost in final coat and decorate (page 98).

Dutch Chocolate
CAKE

Makes 10 servings

CHOCOLATE CAKE

Softened unsalted butter for pans

1¾ cups all-purpose flour, plus more
    for pans

2 cups water

2 cups granulated sugar

¾ cup Dutch-processed cocoa powder

1½ teaspoons baking powder

1½ teaspoons baking soda

2 teaspoons salt

2 large eggs

1 cup milk

½ cup vegetable oil

1 tablespoon vanilla extract

✳ Preheat oven to 350°F. Butter and flour three 8-inch round baking pans. Bring water to a boil. In a stand mixer, combine sugar, flour, cocoa powder, baking powder, baking soda, salt, eggs, milk, oil, and vanilla. Beat on medium speed until smooth. Add 1 cup of the boiling water and beat again on low speed until blended. Divide batter evenly among prepared cake pans. Bake for 35 to 40 minutes, until a toothpick inserted into centers comes out clean.

✳ Remove from oven and allow to cool on racks for 10 minutes before removing from pans. Wrap in plastic and refrigerate until chilled and ready to assemble.

DUTCH CHOCOLATE FROSTING

1¼ cups confectioners' sugar

1½ cups heavy whipping cream

⅓ cup Dutch-processed cocoa powder

1 teaspoon vanilla extract

½ cup shaved dark chocolate or diced
    dark chocolate morsels

✳ In a stand mixer, combine confectioners' sugar, cream, cocoa powder, vanilla, and chocolate. Beat several minutes on high speed until stiff peaks form.

ASSEMBLY

Cake board, cut into a 10-inch circle

Shaved or diced chocolate

✳ Retrieve cakes from fridge. Cut each cake horizontally into two layers. Center first layer on cake board. Spread a generous dollop of chocolate frosting on top and sprinkle with a small handful of shaved or diced chocolate. Top with another cake layer and repeat; continue, using remaining cake layers. Once all layers are stacked, use a serrated blade to carve dome shape. Use remaining chocolate frosting for crumb coat. Chill cake until ready to frost with final coat and decorate (page 98).

Basic White
WEDDING CAKE

Makes 4 servings

This is the smallest of the wedding cakes and is intended to be frozen and enjoyed on the couple's one-year anniversary.

CAKE

½ recipe White Cake (page 4), baked in three 5-inch round cake pans

½ recipe Vanilla Buttercream Frosting (page 6)

ASSEMBLY

Cake board, cut into a 6-inch circle

✳ Retrieve cakes from fridge. Cut each cake horizontally into two layers. Center first layer on cake board. Spread a generous dollop of buttercream on top. Top with another cake layer and repeat; continue, using remaining layers. Once all layers are stacked, use a serrated blade to carve dome shape. Use the remaining buttercream frosting for crumb coat. Chill cake until ready to frost in final coat and decorate (page 98).

Black, red, and yellow food colorings
3 recipes Vanilla Buttercream Frosting
    (page 6)
Royal Icing (page 9)
Modeling Chocolate (page 10)
Brown food coloring (optional)

✳ Use black, red, and yellow food colorings to tint buttercream frosting, creating a beige color. (The amounts of coloring needed vary depending on the brand you go with, so it's best to start off with just a couple drops and mix thoroughly.) Continue until desired color is achieved. Retrieve one cake at a time from fridge and frost with beige-tinted buttercream, putting each cake back in the refrigerator when you're done to chill until buttercream has set. Remove from refrigerator and smooth with water-moistened finger tips.

✳ With a very fine tip, pipe your decorations and create various-size roses with royal icing. (This is just one sentence, but in real life this will take a very, very long time, so be sure to chill your cake in between as necessary!)

✳ To create center medallions on the Hummingbird Cake and the smaller White Wedding Cake, press modeling chocolate into a large soup spoon or serving spoon and allow to set. If you're feeling particularly ambitious, use watered-down royal icing, tinted a light brown, to paint the bride and groom's initials or other personal touches onto the medallions. Adhere to cakes with royal icing.

Ruler or measuring tape

Six 10-inch round wooden disks, at least 1 inch thick

Four 8-inch round wooden disks, at least 1 inch thick

Two 5-inch round wooden disks, at least 1 inch thick

One 25-inch pine table leg

Two 20-inch pine table legs

Two 12-inch decorative columns

One 6-inch decorative column

Twelve 2-inch long wood screws

Nontoxic brown paint or cocoa powder

1½ yards lace trim

Hot-glue gun

Faux pearl strands

✳ Using a ruler or measuring tape, mark center of each wooden disk. Following your marks, screw one 10-inch disk to both ends of 25-inch table leg, one 10-inch disk to both ends of two 20-inch legs, one 8-inch disk to both ends of the two 12-inch columns, and one 5-inch disk to both ends of the 6-inch column.

✳ Paint each stand with brown nontoxic paint, or for a more rustic look, mix equal parts cocoa powder and water and brush on.

✳ Trim lace into three 10½-inch lengths, two 8½-inch lengths, and one 5½-inch length. Hot-glue each length round top edge of each corresponding disk. Hot-glue pearl strands to underside of top disk of 25-inch stand—flip upside down and glue the pearls at 5 to 6 points, leaving 6 to 12 inches of pearls in between; when flipped right side up, this will create a beautiful draped effect.

✳ When ready to present and serve, place each cake on corresponding stand. Pipe white buttercream around edge of each cake to cover any exposed cake board and embellish with buttercream roses.

Earth CAKE

Earth has seen some pretty amazing things in its lifetime. Just like the people who dwell on it, Earth has a life cycle. In its infancy, things were a lot more exciting, from a geological standpoint. But soon afterward, it fell into the routine we've come to appreciate.

Puberty is a tricky time for any planet, and Earth is no exception. Around sixty-six million years ago, our planet was suffering from a severe reptilian infestation and having doubts about its place in the universe. Just then, a comet came hurtling toward it from outer space like a bolt of dino-Clearasil.

Much like a face-lift, things had to get worse before they got better, and the planet went through a slightly less attractive phase. But once the bandages were removed, Earth was rejuvenated and ready to start the next chapter of its life.

There's no telling how long humanity will last before Earth gets fed up again. So here's a cake to remind us all that we're just guests here, and that we need to be cautious of wearing out our welcome!

Earth CAKE

Makes one half-dome planet

1-2-3-4 CAKE

1 cup (2 sticks) unsalted butter, softened, plus more for bowl

3 cups cake flour, plus more for bowl and pans

2½ cups granulated sugar

1½ teaspoons salt

2 teaspoons vanilla extract

½ teaspoon almond extract

4 large eggs

2 teaspoons baking powder

1 cup whole milk

Red and orange food coloring

✳ Preheat oven to 375°F. Butter and flour an ovensafe bowl with an 8-inch rounded bottom and two 8-inch round cake pans.

✳ In a stand mixer, cream together butter, sugar, salt, vanilla, and almond extract. Add eggs one at a time, beating well on medium speed between each addition. Sift flour and baking powder together into a separate bowl. Begin adding to batter, alternating with milk, until all ingredients are combined and smooth.

✳ Set aside one-fourth of batter in a small bowl; divide the remaining batter between two medium bowls. Add red food coloring to one medium bowl and orange food coloring to second medium bowl. Mix until color is uniform throughout. Leave batter in small bowl uncolored (this will be your core). Fill three piping bags, without any tips, with each of the different colored batters.

✳ In your prepared ovensafe bowl, pipe red batter in a thick ring around edge of bowl first (see photo page 104). Follow by piping orange batter into the center.

✳ Grab one of your prepared cake pans and mark where different colored sections should go by scraping a bit of buttered and floured section off bottom of pan. Pipe red batter along outer edge, then a ring of orange inside the red, then a small bit of the pale yellow uncolored batter in the center. Repeat in second cake pan, making the pale center larger. Bake bowl and pans at once for 25 to 30 minutes, until a toothpick inserted into centers comes out clean. Allow to cool on racks for 10 minutes before removing from pans. Wrap each in plastic wrap and chill until ready to assemble.

2 recipes Vanilla Buttercream Frosting (page 6)

Red, yellow, brown, and dark blue food coloring

Royal Icing (page 9)

Small battery-operated flickering "candle" light

Nontoxic tape

Clear piping gel

Granola

✳ Put about ¼ cup of 1 recipe buttercream in a small bowl and lightly tint with yellow food coloring. Of the remaining first batch of buttercream, divide and tint about one-third to a light orange color in a second bowl, and the remaining two-thirds a rich orange-red in a third bowl.

✳ Place bottom cake layer (with red, orange, and yellow sections) onto a serving tray. Spread a layer of yellow buttercream over the yellow section, followed by a ring of light orange, and then a ring of orange-red buttercream. Place second cake layer on top and spread a layer of light orange over the center section, followed by a ring of orange-red buttercream. Top with third, rounded layer from the bowl. Apply crumb coat with remaining orange-red buttercream and refrigerate until firm and fully set.

✳ Tint about one-third of second recipe of buttercream frosting brown and spread a thin layer on cake over crumb coat (for the Earth's crust). Refrigerate until fully set and firm.

✳ Tint about half of remaining buttercream with dark blue food coloring, but do not fully mix—color should *not* be uniform. Frost dome with a thin layer of the marbled blue frosting and refrigerate until fully set and firm. Smooth frosting with water-moistened fingertips and chill again.

✳ Of remaining buttercream, tint one half green and the other a light brown. Once blue frosting layer is very firm, use a brush to paint in the land masses—for each section, add a light brown layer followed by a green layer, blending together in select areas for added realism. Chill cake once more until frosting is fully set and firm.

✳ Using a sharp thin-bladed knife or thin tea-spoon, carve out a circle about 1 inch in diameter and about ½-inch deep where you would like to have your impact site. Using watered-down royal icing and a fine paintbrush, add in the "waves" emanating from the impact site. Add in clouds over the whole cake with the remaining watered-down royal icing and using various brushes—this will vary the texture of the atmosphere for added realism.

✳ Remove exterior of flickering candle light and wrap all components (except top of bulb) in nontoxic tape. Insert light into crater just before serving. Secure light in place with clear piping gel, tinted with orange food coloring. Cover any rough edges with a ring of royal icing. Finish off your masterpiece with a piece of granola for the infamous comet!

Summer

Crab CAKES

To those less cultured, the term "crab cakes" can be very misleading. I did not grow up going to parties on yachts, so you can imagine my surprise when, at the age of twenty-two, I bit into my first crab cake at a friend's house. My mouth was instantly filled with the salty mush that has haunted my dreams ever since. Where was the sugar? Where was the fun? I had been tricked!

When I was a child, I thought Red Lobster was the pinnacle of fine dining. Without much effort, I developed what I like to call "white-trash taste buds." I put ketchup on nearly everything, and believed Miracle Whip lives up to its name. So when I heard the word "cake," I expected something sweet.

Now, as an adult, I have the pleasure of making my own rules. It's the best part of growing up. You can right what you see as wrong and handcraft a life to your choosing. In the world I've made for myself, the animals talk, the birds clean house—and the crabs really are cake!

DISCLAIMER: If your animals are talking to you, please seek emergency services.

Crab
CAKES

Makes 12 crab cakes

WHITE CAKE

¾ cup (1½ sticks) unsalted butter, softened, plus more for pans

3 cups all-purpose flour, plus more for pans

3 cups granulated sugar

¾ cup vegetable shortening

5 large eggs

2 teaspoons baking powder

1 teaspoon salt

½ cup whole milk

½ cup buttermilk

1 tablespoon vanilla extract

✳ Preheat oven to 350°F. Butter and flour two 8-inch round cake pans. In a stand mixer, cream together butter, sugar, and shortening until fluffy. Beat in eggs on medium speed until fully incorporated. In a separate bowl, whisk together flour, baking powder, and salt. Slowly blend dry ingredients into wet ingredients in the mixer. Once fully incorporated, pour in milk, buttermilk, and vanilla. Beat on medium-high speed until fluffy and creamy.

✳ Divide batter evenly between prepared baking pans. Bake for 25 to 35 minutes, until a toothpick comes out clean when inserted into the center of each cake. Allow to cool on racks for 10 minutes before removing from pans. Let cakes cool to room temperature.

✳ Slice each cake horizontally into two layers. Using a 3-inch biscuit cutter or ring mold, cut out six circles from each layer. Set aside until ready to decorate and assemble.

4 cups white melting chocolate
Red food coloring
Yellow food coloring
2 tablespoons light corn syrup

✳ Melt white chocolate over very low heat and add just 1 or 2 drops of red and yellow food coloring at a time until you reach your desired crab color.

✳ Place cake circles over the bottom or side of a rounded glass one at a time, and press edges to give each a domelike effect (see photo page 130).

✳ Dip rounded side of cake disks into pink melted colored chocolate, one at a time, and place on parchment paper, dome-side up. Allow chocolate to fully set. Put half of remaining melted tinted chocolate into a piping bag fitted with an extra-small round tip and pipe little teeth along the perimeter of your cooled and set disks (see photo page 108). Allow to cool and set completely. Place the piping bag in a warm place to prevent the chocolate inside from setting.

✳ Heat remaining pink melting chocolate until it's in a liquid state. Remove from heat and add corn syrup, and stir until modeling chocolate is formed. Cover tightly in plastic wrap and set aside while you make the peach fluff.

PEACH FLUFF

1 package peach-flavored Jell-O,
    prepared according to package
    directions
2 cups heavy whipping cream
3 tablespoons cornstarch
1 teaspoon almond extract
1 (8-ounce) can diced peaches, drained
    and air-dried

✳ Refrigerate Jell-O until firm, about 3 hours. In a stand mixer, beat cream, cornstarch, and almond extract on high speed until stiff peaks form. Fold in peaches. Retrieve Jell-O from refrigerator and scramble it up, using a fork. Fold it into whipped cream mixture. Refrigerate for 1 hour.

✳ ✳ ASSEMBLY & PRESENTATION

Modeling Chocolate, in white
    (page 10)
Modeling Chocolate, in black
    (page 10)
Modeling Chocolate, in yellow
    (page 10)
2 to 3 (2-pound) bags light brown sugar
Vanilla Buttercream Frosting
    (page 6)

✳ Use the set pink modeling chocolate to form the legs and pincers for 12 crabs: For each crab, roll out a 4-inch, a 3½-inch, and a 2-inch strip tapered to points on both ends. Cut each strip in half to create six legs. Sculpt two front claws for each crab. Make twelve sets of eyes out of white and black modeling chocolate. Adhere legs to undersides of twelve of your disks using the melted chocolate in your piping bag. Set aside, legs up, in a cool area until firm and fully set, about 15 minutes. On remaining twelve disks, adhere eyes on your crabs using melted chocolate in piping bag. Add eyebrows behind each eye with yellow modeling chocolate to give adorable pleading expression.

✳ Create a beach scene on your serving tray using brown sugar. Flip your disks so they're now leg-side down and place them on your beach. Fill a piping bag with vanilla buttercream. Using a decorative tip, pipe a ring along the top perimeter of your crabs. Be careful not to cover the teeth you created earlier. Spread a dollop of peach fluff within the buttercream ring on each crab and then rest your tops on the fluff. Place pincers in last and prepare for the ooooo's and AHHHHHH's!

Appalachian

BREAD PUDDING

The Appalachian Mountains are a beautiful and mysterious place, an area so large and dense, much of it has gone unexplored even to this day.

While the northern states have Sasquatch and the southern ones are home to the chupacabra, there is a little-known creature that resides within the thick scrubs and tall trees of these majestic peaks. Most mythic creatures are known for being frightful or terrifying; the reason you may not have heard of this doughy little guy is that he's neither.

Quiet and aloof, these elusive mountain critters have always led a peaceful and tranquil existence. On the rare occasions that they have been spotted, their odd, humanlike form has often been mistaken as the offspring of hill folk who got a little too friendly with their kin, when in fact the folks of this particular region are this creature's greatest ally. Feeding them berries and scraps of crust, the locals have discovered there's only one way to coax these varmints from the shadows—it is, of course, the siren song of the banjo.

Appalachian
BREAD PUDDING

Makes 6 large servings

1 large circular loaf sourdough bread

Softened unsalted butter for pan

All-purpose flour for pan

3 large eggs

5 egg yolks

4 cups half-and-half

1 tablespoon vanilla extract

¾ cup granulated sugar

1 cup raisins

1 cup white chocolate chips

½ cup sliced almonds

1 or 2 sourdough baguettes

✳ Preheat oven to 350°F. On a piece of paper, sketch out the head and hair style you'd like your little guy to have. On sourdough loaf, cut along hairline and perimeter of face. Then pull the bread out, hollowing out loaf. Tear bread into pieces and spread on a rimmed baking sheet. Toast in oven for about 6 minutes, until dry. Set aside until ready to use.

✳ Place hollowed-out bread bowl in a buttered and floured 9-inch round cake pan. In a large bowl, whisk together eggs, yolks, half-and-half, vanilla, and sugar. Stuff bread bowl with toasted bread pieces, raisins (set some aside to use later as decoration), chocolate chips, and almonds, alternating so they're evenly spread throughout. Pour wet ingredients over bread mixture until bread bowl is nearly full. Press contents down until surface is smooth.

✳ Cut one baguette horizontally into long, thin slices of bread to create a light-colored, smooth surface for the face. Lay slices over bread-bowl opening until covered completely. Using an X-Acto knife or other sharp blade, carve features you want to look dark (eyes, nose, mouth, ears) out of baguette crust and place on bread pudding "face." Use squashed raisins for pupils and dark areas of the mouth.

✳ Cover with aluminum foil and bake for 45 minutes. Remove foil and bake for another 45 minutes. Remove from oven and allow to cool before removing from baking dish. You can use a second baguette to create a body and limbs for your little friend, if you like.

GLAZE

2 ounces bourbon
1 cup granulated sugar
½ cup water
1 teaspoon ground cinnamon

✳ In a small saucepan, combine bourbon, sugar, water, and cinnamon. Heat over medium heat until mixture becomes a slightly thick glaze.

ICING

1 cup heavy whipping cream
½ cup confectioners' sugar
1 teaspoon vanilla extract

✳ In a bowl, whisk together cream, confectioners' sugar, and vanilla. To serve, drizzle glaze and icing over sliced pudding just before serving.

Doughnut DINNER

Kids can be picky eaters, and sometimes visually manipulating them is the only way to ensure they're getting the proper amount of nutrition. I'm sure you've seen the McDonald's fries that are actually apple slices or other revoltingly healthy items masquerading as something delicious? Well, I've taken that notion and applied it in my own way by making what's traditionally considered to be a well-rounded meal out of things that would horrify your nutritionist!

If all goes as planned, your kids may be less apprehensive the next time you scoop green beans and carrots onto their plates. It's sort of like my own homespun reverse aversion therapy. Only instead of using something dangerous like an electric shock, you're using glorious amounts of sugar, fat, and carbohydrates.

So try the recipes in the pages that follow to ensure shrieks of joy from your children.

Doughnuts

¼ cup warm water (about 90°F)

2 packets active dry yeast
(1½ tablespoons)

1½ cups whole milk

⅓ cup vegetable shortening

2 large eggs, beaten

⅓ cup granulated sugar, plus more
for rolling

2 teaspoons salt

1 teaspoon ground nutmeg

3 cups all-purpose flour, plus more
for dusting

½ gallon vegetable shortening

✳ Pour water into bowl of a stand mixer; add yeast and allow to bloom, about 5 minutes. In a medium saucepan, heat milk and shortening over low heat until shortening has melted. Pour into yeast mixture. Beat on medium speed until smooth. Add eggs, sugar, salt, and nutmeg. Add 1½ cups of flour, and blend on low speed until fully incorporated. Switch to a dough hook and slowly add remaining flour, mixing until a ball forms. (Note: If dough is too sticky, add a small dusting of flour; if it's too dry, add a splash of water.) Remove and place dough ball in a large oiled bowl, and seal airtight. Let rise in a warm location for about 1½ hours, until doubled in size.

✳ Fill a deep fryer with shortening and heat between 360° and 375°F. Punch dough down, then, on a generously floured surface, roll out dough ball to ¾-inch thickness. Using a sharp blade, cut out fifteen to twenty drumstick shapes.

✳ Line several baking sheets with paper towels and fill a shallow bowl with granulated sugar; place these within reach of fryer. Place drumstick doughnuts two at a time in the deep-fryer tray and lower into hot oil, flipping every few seconds with tongs until dough is golden brown. Remove from fryer and immediately roll in granulated sugar. Set on paper towels to drain briefly (keep oil hot).

FOR THE "CHICKEN SKIN" AND FILLING

6 large eggs, beaten

3 cups all-purpose flour

2 cups canned fruit filling (or jelly),
and/or Bavarian cream

✳ Place eggs in one shallow bowl and flour in a second shallow bowl. For chicken skin appearance, dip doughnut in beaten eggs and then immediately in flour. Repeat one more time and then set in deep fryer for a second time until golden. Remove and allow to cool on clean paper towels. Allow doughnuts to fully cool to room temperature.

✳ Fill a pastry bag with fruit filling or Bavarian cream, and use an injector tip to fill your drumstick doughnuts. (Be careful not to overfill!)

Candy Green Beans & CORN

Makes 10 servings

2 cups green melting chocolate
2 cups yellow melting chocolate
1 (½-pound) bag pretzel sticks
1 cup cornstarch

ADDITIONAL
Toothpicks
2 Styrofoam blocks

✳ Melt green and yellow chocolates separately over very low heat. Pour green chocolate into an ovensafe bowl and yellow chocolate into a pastry bag fitted with an extra-small round tip. Snip tips of about sixty pretzels and insert toothpicks until they just stick.

✳ For the green beans, roll about thirty pretzels in cornstarch until coated, then dip in green melting chocolate. Insert opposite ends of toothpicks into suspended foam block to dry upside-down. Allow to set until hard to the touch before removing toothpicks.

✳ For the corn, pipe small beads along each pretzel in layers until corn appearance is achieved. Stick toothpicks in second foam block to dry, right-side up.

✳ Allow to set until hard to the touch before removing toothpick, then snip off exposed pretzel.

Caramel CARROTS

Makes 10 servings

1 cup (2 sticks) unsalted butter, plus
more for pan
2 cups granulated sugar
1 cup packed light brown sugar
1 cup whole milk
1 cup heavy whipping cream
1 cup light corn syrup
1 teaspoon salt
1 teaspoon vanilla extract
2 cups orange melting chocolate

ADDITIONAL MATERIALS
1-inch round cookie cutter
Ridged carrot slicer
Toothpicks
1 Styrofoam block

✳ Heavily butter a 13 x 18-inch baking tray. In a cast-iron pan, combine granulated sugar, brown sugar, butter, milk, cream, corn syrup, and salt. Heat slowly over medium heat, stirring frequently, until mixture boils and reaches 250°F (use a candy thermometer). Remove from heat, add vanilla, and stir vigorously. Quickly pour caramel into prepared baking tray and allow to cool and set completely.

✳ Melt orange melting chocolate over very low heat and pour into an ovensafe bowl.

✳ Punch out circles from caramel with cookie cutter. Insert a toothpick into edge of each circle about halfway through and place in cool area for a few minutes. Dip circles in orange melting chocolate and then insert other end of toothpicks upright into foam block. Once block is filled, immediately place in freezer until "carrots" are completely set and hard to the touch. Remove from freezer and remove toothpicks.

✳ Carefully heat carrot slicer over a flame and press and slide back and forth against "carrots" to create ridges in chocolate. Set aside until hard to the touch.

ASSEMBLY & PRESENTATION

3 cups vanilla ice cream

½ cup Homemade Caramel sauce
(page 8) or store-bought sauce

✳ Place carrots, green beans, corn, and fried chicken on plates. Scoop vanilla ice cream on plate and finish by drizzling caramel sauce over ice cream to replicate mashed potatoes and gravy!

The Facehugger

Feminism comes in many forms, and is borne for a variety of reasons by different people. My mother grew up in a house predominantly run by women, and when she went out into the work force and found most women taking a back seat, she fought back. She worked hard, and now proudly holds a management position working for the government. She's what I'd call a feminine feminist; she juggles beauty, intimidation, and pantyhose seamlessly.

As the daughter of a feminist, I went in the opposite direction, embracing homemaking and baking, thinking it seemed a much safer world. However, as you can see from the picture to your left, danger is all around us, and you can't just hide behind an apron if you want to survive.

The extraterrestrial species in the movie *Alien* is all about feminism. As a race ruled and governed by a queen, they don't need men—they just need your body!

The
FACEHUGGER

Makes 2 facehugger cookies

SUGAR COOKIES

1½ cups (3 sticks) unsalted butter, softened, plus more for pans

5 cups all-purpose flour, plus more for pans

2 cups granulated sugar

4 large eggs

1 teaspoon vanilla extract

2 teaspoons salt

✳ Preheat oven to 400°F. Butter and flour three baking sheets. In a stand mixer, cream butter and sugar together. Add eggs and vanilla, beating on medium speed. Once smooth, slowly add flour, 1 cup at a time, and finish by adding salt. Divide dough in half. Wrap one half in plastic wrap and set aside. With the other half, you'll be breaking off pieces to mold with clean hands.

✳ This is an extremely time-consuming and delicate project, so keep in mind, the smaller you make your facehuggers, the easier they'll be to construct. This life-size model took two days and a ton of work to create, due to the weight of the cookies. No matter what size you choose, you will need to create: one body, eight legs (with three sections each), one tail, and two round "breathing flaps" (see photo page 131).

✳ For the body, roll out dough on parchment paper or a floured work surface. Sculpt overall shape, using fingers to create indentations and a butter knife or sculpting tool to create score marks. Roll out another section of dough into a log, slightly tapered at one end, about half the length of alien body. Lay log onto body, smoothing tapered end into center of body. Score pattern onto log, then carefully transfer to a prepared baking sheet and place in fridge.

✳ For the tail, roll out more dough into a log, twice the length of body and tapered at one end. (The untapered end should match the diameter of the log already on the body.) Using a butter knife or sculpting tool, add in segmented pattern. Transfer to a prepared baking sheet and slightly curl tapered end.

✳ For the legs, roll out more dough into eight logs. Cut each log into three pieces—lengths will vary depending on the size of your facehugger, but the second and third pieces should be slightly shorter than the preceding piece. For the long and medium sections, indent both ends using fingers. For the shortest section, indent one end and then taper the other to a point. Place on a prepared baking sheet.

✳ For the breathing flaps, roll out more dough to about ¼ inch thick. Cut out two ovals and place over two buttered and floured standard wine glasses. Chill dough on wine glasses until very firm. To help flaps keep their shape while baking, use aluminum foil rolled into a ball and place on prepared baking sheet. Carefully remove flaps from wine glasses and place, dome-side up, over foil balls. With end of a clean paintbrush or a sculpting tool, create an indentation just above widest end of oval. Immediately place in oven.

✳ Bake all alien parts for 8 to 12 minutes, until golden brown, depending on the size of the parts you're baking (body will take longer than other parts).

NOTE: To create a raised tail, immediately shape cookie after removing from oven. Using prepared molds, such as a bowl wrapped in aluminum foil and oiled with cooking spray, is the easiest way to give the tail added shape.

Continued

½ recipe Homemade Caramel
(page 7)

✳ Coat bottoms of each cookie section with caramel and allow to harden. To assemble the aliens, dip one end of a joint in caramel and adhere to opposite joint. Hold until caramel has set. Use wooden skewers to hold various appendages upright until fully constructed.

NOTE: I won't pretend this was an easy project, as you have a very limited amount of time when the caramel will stick. So, if you're brave and decide to tackle this project, be patient and know you'll need to work quickly. A slightly less delicious but much easier method is to use brown royal icing as the glue, allowing each joint to set for at least 5 minutes before moving to the next.

Chocolate Squid GELATIN

So many delicious things come from the sea, but not that surprisingly, they all seem to be on the saltier side. I'm clearly a bigger fan of all things sweet, so for the following recipe, I made a dessert out of what sailors fear most: the dreaded sea squid!

In *20,000 Leagues Under the Sea*, Captain Nemo and his crew face off against a gang of giant squid with devastating consequences. My initial theory was that these creatures were mainly misunderstood— perhaps the *Nautilus* wasn't painted in neutral gang colors? So I decided to make one in my kitchen—to disastrous effect:

#1 They grow a lot faster than you'd think.

#2 They naturally seem to have a crummy disposition.

For those daring enough to try the following recipe at home, I say "Caveat pistor!" To the baker beware . . .

Chocolate Squid GELATIN

BROWNIE BASE

Makes one 10-inch round brownie

¾ cup (1½ sticks) unsalted butter, plus
    more for pan
1¼ cups granulated sugar
¾ cup cocoa powder
½ teaspoon salt
1 teaspoon vanilla extract
2 large eggs, beaten
½ cup all-purpose flour
¾ cup walnuts, toasted and salted

✳ Preheat oven to 325°F. Butter a 10-inch round baking pan. In a medium saucepan over medium heat, melt butter. Add sugar and cocoa and stir until a warm paste forms.

✳ Remove from heat and add salt, vanilla, and eggs. Mix with a wooden spoon until smooth. Add flour and walnuts, and mix until completely blended.

✳ Pour batter into prepared baking pan. Bake for 20 to 25 minutes, until a toothpick inserted into center comes out mostly clean. Allow to cool to room temperature. Chill uncovered in fridge until very firm to the touch, about 2 hours. After chilling, use a biscuit cutter to cut out an even circle in the center for chocolate gelatin to stand in. Cover and refrigerate until ready to assemble.

CHOCOLATE GELATIN

Makes about 3 tall gelatins
½ cup cold water
3 tablespoons unflavored gelatin
    powder, such as Knox
1 cup cocoa powder
1 cup coconut oil
½ cup granulated sugar
½ cup maple syrup
1 tablespoon vanilla extract

1½ cups boiling water

✳ In a stand mixer fitted with whisk attachment, combine ½ cup cold water and gelatin powder. Allow a moment to bloom. Mix cocoa, oil, sugar, syrup, and vanilla into gelatin mixture and whip on medium-high speed until combined. Pour boiling water and whip again until smooth.

✳ Oil three tall parfait glasses and pour in gelatin mixture to tops of glasses. Refrigerate overnight. To release the next day, run warm water over exterior of glasses for just a few moments. Then use a metal tine or skewer up one side of glasses to release the suction. Once removed, invert one gelatin into center of prepared brownie dish.

STABILIZED WHIPPED CREAM OCEAN

1 tablespoon unflavored gelatin powder,
    such as Knox

5 teaspoons water

2 cups heavy whipping cream

¼ cup confectioners' sugar

2 tablespoons cornstarch

✳ Combine gelatin and water in a small saucepan and heat over medium heat until *just* dissolved and hot (do not boil or simmer). Set aside in cool area. In a stand mixer fitted with whisk attachment, begin beating cream on high speed. Add cooled gelatin mixture, sugar, and cornstarch, and beat on high speed until stiff peaks form. Fill a piping bag with whipped cream. Using a tip of your preference, pipe foamy waves on top of brownie base. Refrigerate until whipped cream is fully set.

ASSEMBLY & PRESENTATION

Modeling Chocolate, in dark brown
    (page 10)

✳ Create eyes and tentacles using modeling chocolate. Use round handles of various utensils to shape spiraled tentacles. Use a metal tine or skewer to add holes (suction cups) to tentacles. Once tentacles are set, they can easily be stuck anywhere throughout the whipped cream ocean. For added effect, use a fine round tip on a pastry bag to pipe melted chocolate for menacing eyebrows and the spiral atop the squid's head.

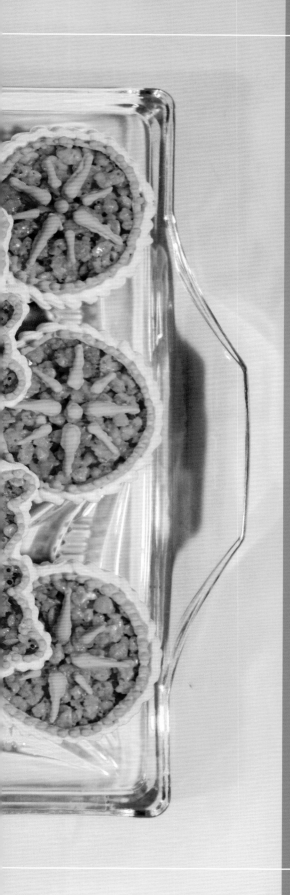

Rice Krispies

BEARS

There are two things I've found to be true in life: Everyone likes a cute teddy bear; and everyone likes Rice Krispies treats!

If you're looking for an adorable, fun, and delicious project to do with the kids, I'd say you can't do one much simpler or cuter than this. It's a perfect way to spend a summer afternoon and the recipe can be adapted for any number of shapes or occassions.

Rice Krispies
BEARS

Makes about 30 treats

¼ cup (½ stick) unsalted butter, plus more for greasing
4 cups miniature marshmallows
5 cups Rice Krispies cereal
Royal Icing (page 9) or white melting chocolate, melted
Food coloring of your choice

✳ In a large pot over medium heat, melt butter and then add marshmallows. Mix for several minutes over low heat until mixture is combined and nice and gooey. Remove from heat and stir in Rice Krispies, using a buttered wooden spoon. Fold over and over until a large ball forms. Wait a few minutes for mixture to cool.

✳ Butter a large cutting board and a rolling pin. Wash and butter hands thoroughly. Roll out Rice Krispies ball into a flat sheet on cutting board roughly ¼ inch thick.

✳ Either use a bear-shaped cookie cutter to create your shapes or draw your own on a piece of card stock and use as a template over rolled-out Krispies. (Hint: you can use the Rice Krispies box for this.)

✳ Once shapes are cut, use royal icing to decorate as you please! If you're a chocolate lover, substitute or add piped melting chocolate.

Peppermint Brownie BUGS

To me, a true brownie is somewhere between cake and fudge and never too far in one direction. When rifling through recipes, finding just the right brownie can be extremely tricky. Luckily, you needn't search any further. This is the brownie recipe to end them all. As much as I'd love to take credit for its invention, I'm afraid the true credit belongs to Alice Medrich. I came across her recipe and, with a few slight alterations and a peppermint insect twist, I can gladly say these are the best brownies I've ever had in my life. Chewy, a bit gooey, and great!

For most people, bugs and desserts rarely go hand in hand, but in this instance, I think they do so adorably. Give them a try, and even if you only make the brownies, I promise that you and anyone within a fifteen-mile radius who smells them will be extremely pleased.

Peppermint
BROWNIE BUGS

Makes about 12 oval brownies

PEPPERMINT BROWNIE

¾ cup (1½ sticks) unsalted butter,
 plus more for pan

1¼ cups granulated sugar

¾ cup cocoa powder

½ teaspoon salt

1 teaspoon vanilla extract

2 large eggs, beaten

½ cup all-purpose flour

¾ cup toasted and salted walnuts

✳ Preheat oven to 325°F. Line a 9-inch square baking dish with parchment paper that extends up the sides, and then thoroughly butter. In a medium saucepan over medium heat, melt butter. Add sugar and cocoa and stir until a warm paste forms. Remove from heat and add salt, vanilla, and eggs. Mix with a wooden spoon until smooth. Add flour and walnuts, and mix until completely blended.

✳ Pour batter into prepared baking dish. Bake for 20 to 25 minutes, until a toothpick inserted into center comes out mostly clean. Allow to cool to room temperature. Remove brownies by pulling on parchment paper. Refrigerate uncovered for at least 1 hour, until chilled and very firm to the touch.

✳ With a sharp knife, cut out brownie bug ovals. Place back in fridge while preparing decorations.

PEPPERMINT CHOCOLATE BODY

1 cup white melting chocolate
¼ cup green melting chocolate
1 teaspoon peppermint extract
2 tablespoons light corn syrup

ADDITIONAL INGREDIENTS
Modeling Chocolate, in dark brown
  and white (page 10)
Edible wafer paper
Black edible ink pen

✳ In a medium saucepan over very low heat, melt both melting chocolates together and add peppermint extract, stirring constantly. When melted, remove from heat.

✳ One by one, take brownie bugs out of fridge and dip bottoms into peppermint chocolate. Place on parchment paper, chocolate-side up, and allow to cool and set.

✳ Reheat remaining peppermint chocolate and add light corn syrup, mixing quickly. (This will create a modeling chocolate you can use for the legs.) Once a ball forms, wrap modeling chocolate in plastic wrap and allow to sit for at least 1 hour before molding.

✳ Use white and dark brown modeling chocolate to make eyes.

✳ To make the wings, use edible black ink to draw wing patterns on edible wafer paper and cut out. Glue wings and eyes onto bug bodies using just a dab of melted brown chocolate.

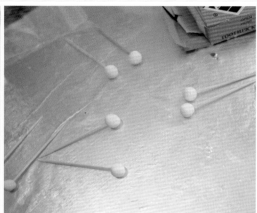

Angel Food Coconut CAT CAKE

Have you ever noticed how some people will brag about the intelligence of their children or their pets? As if these are somehow a reflection of their own intellect? I would say I'm pretty far on the other end of that spectrum.

If you asked one of my elementary school teachers what they thought of me, I doubt the words "bright" or "shows promise" would enter the conversation. My own parents will attest to the fact that nothing great was really expected for my future. In general, I'd call myself a late bloomer, but I actually feel this is one of my greatest strengths. When you're not very bright and are overly optimistic, the world will always be a beautiful and happy place. I think animals with extremely low IQs share the same positive outlook on life.

Therefore, I feel that the dimmest of God's creatures are the real angels on this planet. Which is why I made this delicious coconut angel food cake in the shape of a cat who's clearly a few colors shy of a full box of crayons.

NOTE: I read the text above to my mom before submitting to my editor; her response was "You weren't dumb, you were just uninterested in knowledge."

Angel Food Coconut CAT CAKE

Makes 8 to 10 servings

ANGEL FOOD CAKE

Unsalted butter, softened for pan
1 cup cake flour, sifted, plus more
    for pan
1¾ cups granulated sugar
¼ teaspoon salt
12 egg whites, room temperature
⅓ cup warm water
1 teaspoon vanilla, extract
1½ teaspoons cream of tartar

✳ Preheat oven to 375°F. Butter and flour a standard tube pan. Sift together sugar, salt, and cake flour into a large bowl. In a stand mixer, beat egg whites, water, vanilla, and cream of tartar on high speed until the mixture expands and looks like airy foam. Gently sprinkle flour mixture into wet ingredients and gently whisk by hand, until flour mixture is just incorporated.

✳ Pour batter into prepared tube pan and set on bottom rack of oven. Bake for 30 to 35 minutes; do not open oven until at least the 30-minute mark (cool air will deflate your cake before this time). Remove from oven when top is golden brown and full. Allow to cool at least 1 hour before removing from pan.

PINK COCONUT BUTTERCREAM

1 cup (2 sticks) unsalted butter,
    softened
4 cups confectioners' sugar
1 teaspoon coconut extract
Red food coloring

✳ In a stand mixer, cream butter until smooth. Slowly incorporate confectioners' sugar, 1 cup at a time, and beat on medium speed until fully mixed and light and fluffy. Mix in coconut extract and food coloring to desired shade.

Modeling Chocolate (page 10)
Edible wafer paper
2 cups sweetened shredded coconut
Red food coloring

✳ Remove angel food cake from pan and place on a serving stand or tray. Carve around top edge at an angle to form a dome, reserving cake scraps. Mix scraps with a bit of frosting and shape into two balls for eyes and curved triangles for ears. (If there are more scraps than needed for eyes and ears, use to fill center of cake.) Coat eyeballs with frosting and chill until fully set. Smooth set frosting with water-moistened fingertips. Adhere eyeballs and ears to the cake with additional frosting.

✳ Coat cake with pink frosting and use a bit of modeling chocolate to support ears and to form nose, mouth, and pupils. Cut whiskers out of wafer paper and adhere using frosting. Use red food coloring to tint pink 1½ cups of shredded coconut, and use remaining white coconut on inside of cat's ears. Lightly press pink coconut over rest of head.

Scream BERRIES

Sometimes I come across a new recipe completely by chance. One afternoon, I was overcome with a great desire for an ice-cream cone. So I decided to search online for how to make them at home. Quite a few hours later, this monstrosity was staring back at me.

My point is, if you let your imagination run wild, you're sure to surprise yourself. Creativity doesn't have to make sense every time, and you should never allow the opinions of others to stop you from being daring or ridiculous!

Back to this particular dessert: there was a bright side. It tasted amazing. It's an awesome combination of strawberries, chocolate, cream, and crunch. So if you're in the mood to do something silly and fun, turn the page and create a terrifying dessert sure to brighten any summer day.

Scream BERRIES

Makes 6 servings

CONES

5 tablespoons granulated sugar
¼ cup packed dark brown sugar
1 egg
¼ cup whole milk
2 tablespoons unsalted butter, melted
    and cooled
1 teaspoon vanilla extract
½ cup all-purpose flour

ADDITIONAL
Card stock
Stapler
Aluminum foil
Nonstick cooking spray
8-inch diameter dessert bowl
Filbert brush
Fresh strawberries

✳ Preheat oven to 375°F. Make a mold by cutting out card stock, forming into a cone shape, stapling to hold shape, covering the outside with foil, and then spraying with nonstick cooking spray. Cover dessert bowl with foil and spray with nonstick cooking spray.

✳ Mix sugars with egg in a medium bowl until smooth. Stir in milk, melted butter, and vanilla. Add flour and whisk until smooth and light in color.

✳ On a piece of parchment paper, draw two 5-inch-diameter circles, well spaced, and place on a baking sheet. Using filbert brush, brush batter within lines of your circles slowly and evenly, filling in each circle. Bake for 8 to 12 minutes, until brown. Remove from oven and quickly wrap the circle around cone mold or lay into bowl mold. Allow a few minutes to set. Repeat for remaining batter.

VANILLA MOUSSE

4 cups heavy whipping cream
9 egg yolks
6 tablespoons granulated sugar
2 teaspoons vanilla extract
1 tablespoon salt
½ cup white chocolate chips

✳ Heat cream in a medium saucepan over medium heat. Whisk yolks and sugar together in a heatproof bowl. When cream is hot and just releasing bits of steam, gently temper yolks by *slowly* pouring in 1 cup of hot cream, stirring constantly. Once combined, slowly pour egg mixture back into remaining cream on stovetop, stirring constantly. Heat slowly until just beginning to bubble; remove from heat and add vanilla, salt, and white chocolate. Pour into sealable container and refrigerate for at least 3 hours before piping into cones.

STABILIZED WHIPPED BUBBLES

1 tablespoon unflavored gelatin powder,
    such as Knox
5 teaspoons water
2 cups heavy whipping cream
¼ cup confectioners' sugar
2 tablespoons cornstarch

✳ Combine gelatin and water in a small saucepan over medium heat and stir until *just* dissolved and hot; remove from heat. Begin whipping cream in a stand mixer on high speed. Pour in gelatin mixture, sugar, and cornstarch, and whip until stiff peaks form.

✳ ASSEMBLY & PRESENTATION

Modeling Chocolate, in dark brown
    (page 10)
6 large strawberries
Dark brown melting chocolate, melted
White melting chocolate, melted, or
    Royal Icing (page 9)
Chocolate Cake, crumbled (page 5)

✳ Create tentacles with dark brown modeling chocolate. Cut strawberries in half and glue back together with piped dark brown melting chocolate to resemble open mouths; let cool to set. In a piping bag fitted with an extra-small round tip, pipe melted white chocolate or royal icing for teeth. Let set.

✳ Shortly before serving, fill cones with vanilla mousse, sprinkle with chocolate cake crumbs, and add strawberry monster heads; pipe on whipped cream bubbles to finish.

Mackinac Island FUDGE

Shangri-La is a fictional place in James Hilton's 1933 novel *Lost Horizon* and is described as paradise on earth. For me, such a place actually exists, and is just a short flight and ferry ride away. The place I speak of is as frozen in time as anywhere can be. The sounds of automobiles and buses are replaced by the clacking of horses' hooves. The only smells in the air are of chocolate from the many storefronts specializing in homemade fudge and ice cream. The place I'm talking about is Mackinac Island in Michigan.

Isolated and beautiful, this Neverland is home to the most beautiful structure I've ever visited: the Grand Hotel. It's also the backdrop of one of my favorite movies, *Somewhere in Time*. The entire island is so calm and tranquil, it feels like it can't be real. Essentially it's home to everything I love about life: old structures; Midwestern foliage; and sweets, sweets, and more sweets.

My dream is to someday buy a house here and spend my golden years rocking gently on the porch of the Grand Hotel, eating my body weight in fudge daily. But since those days seem far away at the moment, I decided to create a sculpture of my dream life made of the very thing that I hope one day kills me.

Chocolate
FUDGE

Makes about 4 cups

4 cups granulated sugar

1 cup cocoa powder

2 cups whole milk

½ cup (1 stick) unsalted butter, cut into pieces

1 tablespoon vanilla extract

1 cup walnut pieces, toasted and salted

✳ In a deep, heavy-bottomed pot, combine sugar, cocoa powder, and milk. Heat over medium heat, stirring until mixture comes to a boil. Reduce heat slightly and clip a candy thermometer on inside of pot. Do not stir again. When mixture reaches 236°F, remove from heat. Pour into a large bowl, making sure not to scrape sides. Using a wooden spoon, mix in butter and beat by hand. After butter is fully incorporated, add vanilla and nuts.

✳ (If you just want the fudge without using it for sculpting, simply pour into a 10-inch square baking pan lined with parchment and refrigerate for an hour until set, then enjoy.) Continue mixing by hand until a large ball is formed. Then, using clean hands, remove and mold to desired shape.

NOTE: The base of this sculpture was made by making 4 batches of this recipe.

White Chocolate FUGDE

Makes about 4 cups

¾ cup (1½ sticks) unsalted butter, plus more for pan

3 cups granulated sugar

1 (5-ounce) can evaporated milk

1 teaspoon salt

10 to 12 ounces white chocolate, chopped

1 (8-ounce) jar marshmallow cream

2 teaspoons vanilla extract

✳ Butter a 13 x 18-inch rimmed baking sheet and line with parchment paper. In a heavy-bottomed pot over medium heat, combine butter, sugar, evaporated milk, and salt. Heat to a boil, stirring constantly. Boil for a few minutes, then remove from heat and add white chocolate, marshmallow cream, and vanilla. Beat with a wooden spoon until smooth and blended. Pour into prepared pan and allow to set on the counter or in fridge. After completely set, about 1 hour, you can either eat right away or use for sculpting.

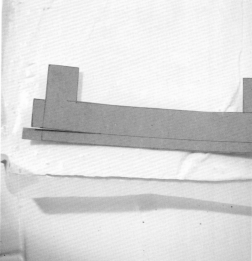

Cream Cheese FUDGE

Makes about 4 cups

½ cup (1 stick) unsalted butter, softened
1 (8-ounce) package cream cheese
4 cups confectioners' sugar
2 teaspoons vanilla extract
1 tablespoon heavy whipping cream

✳ In a stand mixer, cream together butter and cream cheese until smooth. Blend in confectioners' sugar, 1 cup at a time. Once incorporated, add vanilla and cream and beat until smooth.

✳ ASSEMBLY & DECORATION ✳

Paperboard or thin cardboard
Edible black paint
12 ounces white melting chocolate
12 ounces light green melting chocolate
12 ounces dark green melting chocolate
12 ounces dark brown melting chocolate
Green and dark blue food coloring
Vanilla Buttercream Frosting (page 6)
Corn syrup

✳ To construct the landscape, on a 14 x 18-inch cake board, mold chocolate fudge into a rectangle with a roughly semicircle shape at one end, about 2 to 3 inches high. Once fully set and cooled to room temperature, carve fudge to refine shape as shown.

✳ For the hotel, make a stencil using paperboard or thin cardboard. Use stencil to cut out multiple layers from white chocolate fudge. Stack white chocolate fudge into general shape of building, about 2 inches high, and then carve to refine.

✳ Using a toothpick or sharp blade, lightly score fudge to mark out where windows will be, evenly spaced. With a fine paintbrush and edible black paint, add in windows.

✳ For porch columns, use a ruler to draw at least twenty-five 2-inch lines and four 1-inch lines on a sheet of parchment paper (more to account for breakage). Place parchment paper on a baking sheet. In a small saucepan, melt white chocolate until it reaches a liquid state. Transfer about half of white chocolate to a piping bag fitted with a medium round tip. Pipe porch columns onto parchment paper and set aside to fully set. Meanwhile, switch to a small round tip to pipe window frames.

✳ Once columns have set, use more melted white chocolate to adhere to fudge structure. Pipe in remaining porch details.

NOTE: The remaining white chocolate can be separated into multiple batches and mixed with food colorings to create pink, yellow, and red accents for flowers and lower-level window accents, once the foliage has been added in.

✳ For the front lawn, use green food coloring to color a small portion of buttercream. Spread over a thin layer in front of hotel and allow to partially set. Create a cross-hatch pattern using a fine paintbrush and allow to fully set.

✳ For the foliage, melt down light green, dark green, and dark brown chocolates in separate saucepans. Transfer each chocolate to separate pastry bags with various decorative tips. Alternate between the three colors to build up foliage around chocolate fudge base.

✳ For the lake, add dark blue food coloring to a small portion of remaining buttercream. Partially mix, but do not fully incorporate—color should *not* be uniform throughout. Spread a thin layer onto front portion of fudge base. Just before presenting and serving, brush over with a dollop of corn syrup for a glassy water effect.

Dragon Bee

LEMON BARS

When life gives you lemons, I say make lemon bars! These delicious treats have such a great flavor, you'll find yourself bombarded by those seeking the recipe. Luckily for everyone who likes lemons, it's incredibly easy.

I started using this particular recipe several years ago and have personally fine-tuned it to perfection. These have the perfect amount of crunch and zing. They also freeze beautifully, should you need several on a lazy hot summer day. They're also the perfect treat to bring to a barbecue or picnic.

Dragon Bee
LEMON BARS

Makes 8 bars

CRUST

1 cup (2 sticks) unsalted butter,
    softened, plus more for pan
2 cups all-purpose flour, plus more
    for pan
½ cup granulated sugar

* Preheat oven to 350°F. Butter and flour a rimmed 10 x 14-inch baking sheet. In a medium bowl, combine butter, sugar, and flour, using a pastry cutter. Mix until just uniformly crumbly. Spread dough evenly on prepared baking sheet, pressing flat. Bake for 10 to 15 minutes, until just starting to brown.

FILLING

4 large eggs, beaten
1½ cups granulated sugar
¼ cup all-purpose flour
¼ cup grated lemon zest
Juice of 3 lemons
Yellow food coloring
Confectioners' sugar for dusting

* In a medium bowl, combine eggs, sugar, flour, lemon zest, lemon juice, and food coloring and stir until smooth. Pour over toasted crust, place back in oven, and bake for about 20 minutes, until edges just brown.

* Remove from oven and allow to cool. Dust with confectioners' sugar. Use a 2-inch round pastry cutter to cut out twenty-four circles. Stack three circles on top of each other to create eight stacks. Use a heated metal sculpting tool or skewer (I used one in the shape of a hexagon, but a round or circular end will work as well) to create the honeycomb indentations. Place stacked bars, evenly spaced, on a rimmed baking sheet and set aside.

HONEY MERINGUE

3 egg whites
½ teaspoon cream of tartar
¾ cup granulated sugar
1 tablespoon honey

* Preheat oven to 200°F. In a stand mixer with whisk attachment, beat egg whites with cream of tartar on high speed until airy and fluffy. Slowly add granulated sugar, allowing each addition to blend completely before incorporating more. Whip on high speed until stiff and glossy peaks form, then beat in honey last. Scoop into a pastry bag with a large round tip and pipe the tops of your lemon bars in a rising spiral pattern. Set baking sheet in oven, leaving door open to allow meringues to dry-toast, about 45 minutes to an hour. Finished meringues will be hard to the touch and have small visible cracks throughout.

Vanilla Buttercream Frosting
(page 6)
Yellow food coloring
½ cup white melting chocolate, melted

✳ For the dragon bees, tint half of the buttercream with yellow food coloring. Pipe bodies using a round tip onto dry baked meringue. Pipe back scales on bees and add decoration to bars' edges using piped untinted buttercream. The wings and legs were made by piping melting chocolate onto waxed paper. Once completely cooled, adhere to buttercream body.

Fall

Salted Caramel
APPLE PIE

There is no social event in the world where an apple pie isn't welcome. Whether you want to cheer up an old friend or remind your kids why you're #1, apple pie is the way to go.

It's hard tinkering with perfection, but I like to put my own spin on things, even the classics. Salted caramel became immensely popular a number of years ago, and if you've tried it, you know why. Just the thought of the creamy, buttery taste of caramel sprinkled with cracked salt can get your mouth watering.

So if you've got an afternoon off and want to have some fun, give this recipe a try. You won't regret it!

Salted Caramel
APPLE PIE

Makes 8 servings

PIE CRUST

2½ cups all-purpose flour, plus more
    for dish
3 tablespoons granulated sugar
½ teaspoon salt
¼ cup cold vegetable shortening
14 tablespoons (1¾ sticks) cold unsalted
    butter, cubed, plus more for dish
½ cup ice water

EGG WASH
1 large egg
2 tablespoons whole milk

✳ Mix flour, sugar, and salt in a large bowl. Using a pastry cutter, mix in shortening until uniformly crumbed. Cut in cold cubed butter until mixture is chunky. Then mix in water until a rough dough forms, and form into two balls. Flatten balls into individual disks, wrap in foil, and refrigerate for 1 hour.

✳ Preheat oven to 415°F. Butter and flour a large pie dish. Take one disk out of fridge and roll out to ⅛-inch thickness on a floured surface; lay it in dish. Combine egg and milk for egg wash and brush a coat over bottom crust and edge. (Sprinkle with a little sugar, if you like.)

PIE FILLING

7 Granny Smith apples, cored, peeled,
    and thinly sliced
¼ cup fresh lemon juice
½ cup (1 stick) unsalted butter
¾ cup granulated sugar
½ cup packed light brown sugar
6 tablespoons all-purpose flour
¼ cup water
1 cup pecans, salted and toasted

✳ In a large bowl, toss apples with lemon juice. Cover with plastic wrap and set aside. In a medium saucepan over medium heat, melt butter with sugars and flour. Mix in water and bring to a boil. Reduce heat and allow to simmer a few minutes more, then remove from heat.

✳ Chop half of the toasted pecans, and set near pie dish. Arrange apples on crust in pie dish, sprinkling in chopped pecans in as you go. Pour filling butter mixture over apples.

✳ Remove second dough disk from fridge, roll out to ⅛-inch thickness on a floured surface, and cut out tree design with a sharp blade. Lay this design delicately on top of pie. Cut out any remaining rolled dough into small leaf shapes. Place decoratively over tree and along edges of pie (except for the tree trunk). Carefully baste top with remainder of egg wash.

✳ Bake for 15 minutes. Reduce heat to 350°F and bake for another 45 to 55 minutes. If edges brown too quickly, cover with foil and rotate pie. Finished pie should look evenly golden and apple filling should be bubbling through openings. Remove from oven and allow to cool for at least 30 minutes.

SALTED CARAMEL TOPPING

¼ cup (½ stick) unsalted butter, plus more for pan

1 cup heavy cream

2 tablespoons coarse sea salt, plus more for "apples"

1 ½ cups granulated sugar

¼ cup corn syrup

¼ cup water

½ teaspoon vanilla extract

✳ Butter a 13 x 18-inch baking tray lined with parchment paper. In a medium saucepan over medium heat, melt butter with cream and salt. Set aside.

✳ In a large saucepan, mix sugar, corn syrup, and water until a paste forms. Using a candy thermometer, heat mixture until it reaches 250°F—do not exceed 300°F. Mix in butter and cream mixture and heat until boiling. Cook until mixture becomes an amber caramel color, then remove from heat and quickly whisk in vanilla. Pour mixture into prepared baking tray and allow to set, about 20 minutes.

✳ Pinch off bits of caramel with clean hands and roll into pea-size balls. Sprinkle balls with freshly ground sea salt and strategically place on completely cooled pie.

Harvest Wedding CAKE

My brother got married last fall and asked me to bake his wedding cake. When you look at the two of us together, it's fairly astonishing that we both at one time called the same womb home. He's into beer, baseball, and beer. I'm into cats, crocheting, and *Dynasty*. So when he said he wanted something that looked down-home and country, I had to revise my style, which actually turned out to be a lot of fun!

Sometimes stepping out of your comfort zone can be an awesome way to discover another (albeit grimier) side of yourself. My brother's now-wife is not a big fan of frosting and requested a rustic, naked cake. This is a fairly new style, and I've got to tell you, it has a fan base for a reason! The simple technique is a wonderful way for an amateur cake baker to really create something delicious and beautiful.

It starts out like any other cake: with flour, eggs, and fun. But it's when you take it out of the oven that this new style branches off in another direction. A variety of fillings can be used between layers, and embellishments really run the gamut. I once made one with raspberry preserves spread between layers of fresh white cake, decorated with actual berries, grapes on the vine, and some plum-colored roses dusted with powdered sugar for a beautiful and feminine effect.

My brother's wedding cake was tricky because his bride wanted a variety of cake flavors as well. So I needed to be inventive. I ended up creating three species of cake: pumpkin-vanilla, peanut butter–chocolate, and maple-bacon. All turned out delicious, and were big hits!

Pumpkin-
VANILLA

Makes one 2-layer 18-inch cake and one 2-layer 5-inch cake

WHITE CAKE

NOTE: The ingredients below are enough to create one 18-inch layer and one 5-inch layer. Unless you have an industrial-size mixer, you'll need to make the batter for each cake's two layers separately.

¾ cup (1½ sticks) unsalted butter, softened, plus more for pans
3 cups all-purpose flour, plus more for pans
¾ cup vegetable shortening
3 cups granulated sugar
5 eggs
2 teaspoons baking powder
1 teaspoon salt
½ cup whole milk
½ cup buttermilk
1 tablespoon vanilla extract

✳ Preheat oven to 350°F. Butter and flour two 18-inch and two 5-inch round cake pans. In a stand mixer, cream together butter, shortening, and sugar. Beat in eggs on medium-high speed until smooth.

✳ In a separate medium metal bowl, mix flour, baking powder, and salt. Blend dry mixture a little at a time into batter in mixer until combined. Pour in milk, buttermilk, and vanilla, beating on medium-high speed until fluffy and creamy.

✳ Pour into one 18-inch and one 5-inch prepared baking pan and bake for 35 to 40 minutes, until a toothpick inserted into centers comes out clean. Allow to cool for 10 minutes before removing from pans, then allow to cool to room temperature. Repeat for second 18-inch and 5-inch layers.

PUMPKIN BUTTERCREAM

½ cup (1 stick) unsalted butter, softened
1 cup canned pumpkin pie filling
5 cups confectioners' sugar
1 teaspoon vanilla extract
1 teaspoon ground cinnamon
¼ teaspoon ground nutmeg

✳ In a stand mixer, cream together butter and pie filling. Incorporate confectioners' sugar, 1 cup at a time, beating until stiff peaks form. Add vanilla, cinnamon, and nutmeg and fully incorporated.

✳ ✳ ASSEMBLY & PRESENTATION

Cake board, cut into one 5-inch
    and one 18-inch round circle
Miniature pumpkins
Cinnamon sticks
Vanilla beans
Whole cloves
Confectioners' sugar

✳ Center one 5-inch and one 18-inch layer on corresponding cake boards. Spread pumpkin buttercream generously on top; add second layers to each and spread with frosting. Garnish with miniature pumpkins, cinnamon sticks, vanilla beans, and cloves. Dust with confectioners' sugar.

Peanut Butter— CHOCOLATE

Makes one 2-layer 8-inch cake and one 2-layer 14-inch cake

BASIC CHOCOLATE CAKE

2 cups water

Unsalted butter, softened, for pans

4 cups all-purpose flour, plus more
     for pans

4 cups granulated sugar

1½ cups cocoa powder

1 tablespoon baking powder

1 tablespoon baking soda

1 tablespoon salt

4 eggs

2 cups whole milk

1 cup vegetable oil

2 tablespoons vanilla extract

✳ Preheat oven to 350°F. Put water on the stove to boil. Butter and flour two 14-inch and two 8-inch round cake pans.

✳ In a stand mixer, combine on medium speed sugar, flour, cocoa powder, baking powder, baking soda, salt, eggs, milk, vegetable oil, and vanilla. Blend until smooth. Pour in boiling water and mix immediately on low speed.

✳ Divide batter among prepared cake pans and bake for 30 to 40 minutes, until a toothpick inserted into centers comes out clean. Allow to cool for 10 minutes before removing from pans onto racks. Let cool to room temperature.

PEANUT BUTTERCREAM

½ cup (1 stick) unsalted butter, melted

1 cup smooth peanut butter

3 cups confectioners' sugar

½ teaspoon salt

✳ In a stand mixer, cream together butter and peanut butter. Mix in confectioners' sugar, 1 cup at a time, and beat until stiff peaks form. Incorporate salt.

Cake board, cut into one 14-inch
circle and one 8-inch circle
Peanuts in the shell
Chocolate shavings
Chocolate chips
Cocoa powder for dusting

✳ Cut each cake horizontally into two layers. Center one 8-inch and one 14-inch cake on corresponding cake boards. Spread peanut buttercream generously on top of layers and repeat with remaining layers as you stack your cakes. Garnish with peanuts (in the shell), chocolate shavings, and chocolate chips. Dust with cocoa powder.

Maple
BACON

Makes one 2-layer 10-inch cake

MAPLE CAKE

1 cup (2 sticks) unsalted butter, soft-
    ened, plus more for pans
2½ cups all-purpose flour, plus more
    for pans
1 cup maple syrup
½ cup granulated sugar
2 eggs
1½ teaspoons baking powder
1½ teaspoons baking soda
1 teaspoon salt
1 cup sour cream
2 teaspoons vanilla extract

✳ Preheat oven to 350°F. Butter and flour two 10-inch round cake pans. In a stand mixer, beat butter, syrup, and sugar on medium-high speed until light in color. Then beat in eggs, one at a time. In a separate medium bowl, combine flour, baking powder, baking soda, and salt and whisk. Slowly blend dry ingredients into wet ingredients until just combined; gently mix in sour cream and vanilla.

✳ Divide batter evenly between prepared pans and bake for 35 to 45 minutes, until a toothpick inserted into centers comes out clean. Allow to cool for 10 minutes before removing from pans onto racks. Let cool to room temperature.

MAPLE BUTTERCREAM

½ cup (1 stick) unsalted butter,
    softened
½ cup maple syrup
3 cups confectioners' sugar
1 teaspoon salt

✳ In a stand mixer, cream together butter and syrup on medium-high speed until smooth. Incorporate confectioners' sugar, 1 cup at a time. Mix in salt and blend on medium speed until smooth.

ASSEMBLY & PRESENTATION

1 pound maple bacon
Coarse salt
Cake board, cut into a 10-inch circle
Light brown sugar

✳ While cake layers are cooling, preheat oven to 450°F. Empty a pack of maple bacon onto a rimmed baking sheet and spread slices out. Dust with coarse salt and bake until color is deep and texture is crispy; baking time can vary, so keep an eye on the bacon after 15 minutes. Remove and allow to cool to room temperature, then break into some large and some small bits.

✳ Slice each cooled maple cake horizontally into two layers. Center one layer on cake board. Spread a generous dollop of maple buttercream on top, and sprinkle with bacon bits; repeat with remaining layers. Garnish with brown sugar in clumps with shards of bacon resting here and there.

FINAL ASSEMBLY: THE CAKE STAND

I built this tiered cake stand using only wood and nails and then painted it with a mixture of equal parts water and cocoa powder. It's simple but really added to the desired rustic presentation. Challenge yourself to build your own cake stand and add another skill to your artistic arsenal.

Pumpkin
ICE CREAM

I think I may be addicted to ice cream. This diabetes-inducing love affair started several years ago with simple gateway flavors like vanilla and chocolate; but then one thing led to another, and I found myself dabbling in Moose Tracks and then escalating to Ben & Jerry's. I now find myself fantasizing about one flavor while actively eating another.

They say variety is the spice of life, and I'm inclined to agree with them when it comes to my favorite frozen treat. This year I came across a flavor so good, it's now within my top three. Want to know the best part? You can make it at home—and thanks to nature, it comes with its own special container.

Pumpkin ice cream hasn't been around forever, and I feel sadness for generations that have come and gone without having experienced it. The taste is completely unique, and eating a small portion is never enough. I'll warn you now, this recipe is time-consuming (it spans several days). However, if done right, the end result is so creamy and smooth, with such a habit-forming flavor, you may find yourself living on the street and selling off family jewels for pumpkin money.

Pumpkin ICE CREAM

4 cups fresh pumpkin purée (canned pumpkin purée can be substituted, but be sure to procure 100% pumpkin purée with no added spices)

2 tablespoons vanilla extract

8 cups heavy whipping cream

3½ cups packed dark brown sugar

20 egg yolks

2 teaspoons ground cinnamon

2 teaspoons ground ginger

2 teaspoons salt

½ cup bourbon

Whipped cream for garnish

Cinnamon sticks for garnish

ADDITIONAL

1 small to large pumpkin (see Note)

Ice-cream maker

NOTE: I tripled this recipe in order to fill my large pumpkin, but a single recipe is enough for a smaller pumpkin.

✳ Start the night before by mixing pumpkin and vanilla together in a large bowl and refrigerating, covered, overnight. The next morning, heat 6 cups of heavy cream with brown sugar in a large pot over medium heat. In a separate bowl, mix remaining 2 cups heavy cream, yolks, spices, and salt.

✳ Pour 1 cup hot cream into yolk mixture, whisking constantly, slowly allowing eggs to temper. Once thoroughly combined, slowly pour yolk mixture back into cream mixture, stirring slowly and constantly. Continue to heat at a simmer, stirring constantly, until mixture begins to thicken, about 5 minutes. Remove from heat.

✳ Remove pumpkin mixture from fridge and pour into cream mixture, along with bourbon. Whisk thoroughly until creamy and smooth. Seal in an airtight container and refrigerate till the next morning. (The time spent in the refrigerator allows the pumpkin purée to fully bloom and allows for a smoother ice cream.)

✳ The night before you finish making your ice cream, carve thin decorative shapes on the surface of your pumpkin, being careful not to puncture all the way through (as this is your container). I traced my pattern onto the pumpkin first to make things a bit easier. Cut out a lid from the top of your pumpkin. Empty pumpkin of seeds and pulp, and clean thoroughly. Once done, place in freezer overnight.

✳ The next morning, plug in your ice-cream maker and, 3 cups at a time, begin making ice cream. Once each batch is done, scoop ice cream into frozen pumpkin until completely full, and freeze for at least 8 hours.

✳ When serving, top off with whipped cream and a cinnamon stick for a beautiful and flavorful presentation.

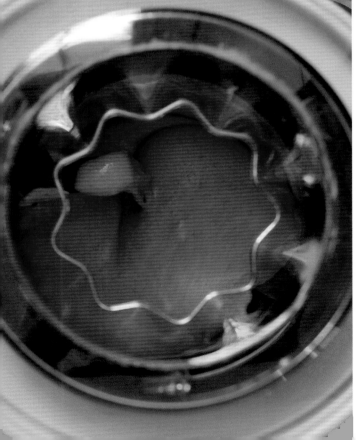

Mint Chip
MEDUSA CAKE

I'll admit that combining this mythological creature and my favorite ice cream flavor is an odd combination for a cake. That said, it really rolls off the tongue, and the colors are so complementary!

Medusa originated in Greek mythology as an evil monster that could turn her victims to stone with a single glance. With hair composed of serpents and an overall bad attitude, she earned enough enemies to end up being beheaded. I wonder though, had she gotten a proper blowout and invested in some specialty eyewear, would things have worked out differently? Perhaps a slice of this cake could have turned her frown upside down?

I suppose we'll never know, but that shouldn't stop you from trying out this next recipe. It may not actually have Medusa's powers, but if you eat enough of it, you may find yourself in a food coma—which is kind of like stone, I suppose.

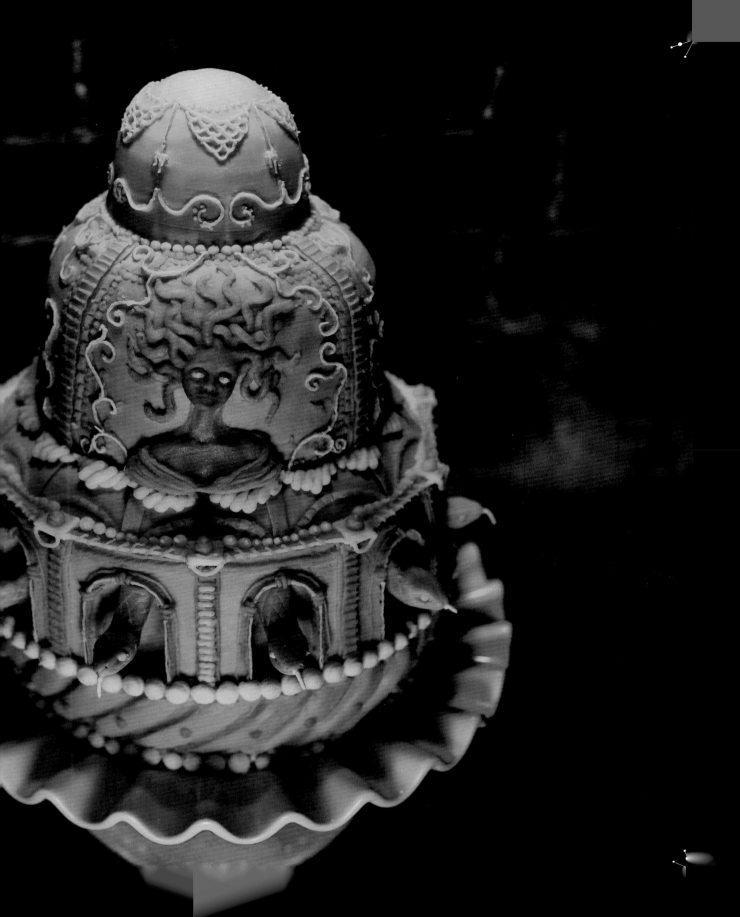

Mint Chip
MEDUSA CAKE

Makes one 8-layer cake

MINT CHIP CAKE

2 cups (4 sticks) unsalted butter, softened, plus more for pans

6 cups all-purpose flour, plus more for pans

1 cup vegetable shortening

6 cups granulated sugar

10 eggs, room temperature

4 teaspoons baking powder

2 teaspoons salt

1 cup whole milk, room temperature

1 cup buttermilk, room temperature

2 tablespoons vanilla extract

4 teaspoons peppermint extract

Several drops of green food coloring

2 cups chocolate chips

✳ Preheat oven to 350°F. Butter and flour two 10-inch, four 8-inch, and two 5-inch round cake pans. In a stand mixer, combine butter, shortening, and sugar. Beat on medium-high speed until fluffy. Add eggs, one at a time, beating between each addition. Beat until very fluffy.

✳ In a separate bowl, combine flour, baking powder, and salt. In a third bowl, combine whole milk, buttermilk, and vanilla. Add flour and milk mixtures to batter, beating until combined; stir in food coloring and peppermint extract. Divide batter evenly among prepared cake pans. Sprinkle in chocolate chips and, using a fork, submerge all exposed chips.

✳ Bake for 25 to 35 minutes, until a toothpick inserted into centers comes out clean and tops are just browned. Remove from oven and allow to cool for 10 minutes before removing from pans. Promptly wrap in plastic and refrigerate until chilled before assembly.

MINT FROSTING

1 cup (2 sticks) unsalted butter, softened

4 cups confectioners' sugar

1 teaspoon vanilla extract

2 teaspoons peppermint extract

Several drops of green food coloring

1 tablespoon heavy whipping cream

✳ In a stand mixer, cream butter. Slowly add confectioners' sugar, 1 cup at a time, beating on medium speed until light and fluffy. Add vanilla, peppermint extract, food coloring, and cream. Beat until fully incorporated.

Vanilla Buttercream Frosting
(page 6)
Green food coloring
Modeling Chocolate, in green
(page 10)
Paintbrush or other sculpting tools

✳ Remove cakes from fridge and slice each cake horizontally into two layers. Center one 10-inch layer on a serving tray. Spread with a generous dollop of mint frosting and top with second 10-inch layer. Continue alternating between cake and frosting layers as you stack remaining 10-inch, 8-inch, and finally your 5-inch layers.

✳ Create the rounded dome shape of each section using a serrated blade to trim top edges at an angle. Using a small sharp knife or small melon baller, carve out 8 to 10 archways, about ¼-inch deep and evenly spaced around the bottom cake section.

✳ Use more mint frosting to apply crumb coat and then place in the refrigerator to chill. Once crumb coat has set, frost in final layer of mint frosting and chill again. Once fully set, remove from refrigerator and use water-moistened fingertips to smooth frosting.

✳ Reserve a small portion of vanilla buttercream and set aside. Tint the rest with green food coloring to desired shade and place in a pastry bag with a small round tip; pipe the general head and bust shape of a Medusa. If necessary, chill again before shaping features with a water-moistened paintbrush or other sculpting tools of your choice. Allow head and bust to fully set before piping on hair and dress top. Switch tips and pipe decorations around archways and bottom and middle cake sections with green buttercream. Chill cake once more until frosting has set.

✳ Meanwhile, use green modeling chocolate to create serpent heads for each archway. Once you have the general shape, stick a toothpick partway into the end of each serpent's "neck." Sculpt the eyes and then use the end of another toothpick to create the nose, mouth, and scored scales. Allow modeling chocolate to fully set before inserting into the cake via the toothpicks.

✳ Finally, use plain vanilla buttercream to pipe the white accent details.

 Poison Apple
PUNCH

I love children. They are sweet, happy, and radiate health and vitality. This is usually attributed to their young age and lack of stress and hardships. However, I believe they are tapping that peachy skin and glossy hair from a slightly more ominous well: their parents. Having children ages you, and while your spawn grows taller and stronger, your bones begin to weaken and your resilience fades. Obviously, we age even if we choose not to reproduce, but children have a supernatural ability to speed up this natural process and slowly siphon off your life force.

But there is a solution. It's a slightly unethical one but, when put to good use early on, will save years on your face. It's generally considered bad parenting to drug or otherwise subdue your children by chemical means ... but what if it's a substance made by Mother Nature herself?

There are two things children universally love: fairy tales and sugar. The following recipe combines both to create something guaranteed to initially enchant them and then shortly thereafter send them into a near-diabetic coma—or, as I like to call it, nap time.

This will give you hours more to primp and pluck your way back to your most attractive self!

Poison Apple
PUNCH

Makes 6 to 8 servings

1 (15-ounce) carton lime sherbet

5 glossy red apples, washed

1 (2-liter) bottle 7-Up

5 green glow sticks, washed

2 pounds dry ice

✳ Scoop at least half of the sherbet into a punch bowl (use more if you'd like). Core and slice apples in half and drop in. Pour in the 7-Up (or clear, carbonated drink of your choosing). Once the kids are near, bend glow sticks, just till they crack inside; don't puncture or break exterior case (you want to drug the children with sugar, not kill them with poison) and drop them in. As the last step, put on some gloves and break off a few chunks of dry ice and plop them in. The effect is dazzling, and guaranteed to have all the kids talking excitedly before slipping off to dream land.

NOTE: Dry ice can be hard to find. I picked mine up at a local ice-cream supply distributor. It doesn't cost much, and I suggest buying more than you need because it's fun to play with. (But make sure to follow safety instructions for handling!)

Sugar Cookie GRAVEYARD

People like roller coasters, horror movies, and haunted carnivals because there is a thrill in being scared. In a way, you're making a joke out of your greatest fears, and I think that's a wonderful thing. What I've done with this next recipe is combine something people love with something they dread.

Graveyards and cookies may seem like an odd mix, but when combined for a centerpiece at a Halloween party, it's a match made in . . . well, a graveyard. But seriously, I made this for a friend's party and it was a huge hit. Nothing sets the tone better for a celebration than reminding all your guests that they're going to die someday—and that it's okay, because you made brownies and sugar cookies!

This is a really fun party recipe to make with a few friends, or your kids. The components are simple and can all be made the day before. I've also found that playing your favorite Halloween movie in the background while you work really gets you in the mood!

Sugar Cookie GRAVEYARD

BROWNIE GRAVEYARD

Makes two 10 x 14-inch sheets

1½ cups (3 sticks) unsalted butter, softened, plus more for pan

1½ cups all-purpose flour, plus more for pan

3 cups granulated sugar

6 eggs

4 teaspoons vanilla extract

1 cup cocoa powder

1 tablespoon salt

1½ teaspoons baking powder

2 cups chocolate chips

✳ Preheat oven to 350°F. Butter and flour two 10 x 14-inch rimmed baking sheets. In a stand mixer, cream together butter and sugar. Add eggs and vanilla and beat on medium-high speed until creamy. In a separate bowl, whisk together cocoa powder, flour, salt, and baking powder. Slowly incorporate dry ingredients into wet ingredients and mix until smooth. Stir in chocolate chips. Divide batter between prepared baking sheets. Bake for 15 to 20 minutes, until a toothpick inserted into centers comes out mostly clean. Allow to cool to room temperature. Repeat until all batter is used (it will yield plenty of brownie to work with).

SUGAR COOKIE TOMBSTONES

Makes two dozen cookies

1½ cups (3 sticks) unsalted butter, softened, plus more for pan

5 cups all-purpose flour, plus more for pan

2 cups granulated sugar

4 eggs

1 teaspoon vanilla extract

2 teaspoons salt

ADDITIONAL

Card stock

✳ Draw tombstone shapes on card stock, then cut out to use as templates. Preheat oven to 400°F. Butter and flour a large baking sheet. In a stand mixer, cream together butter and sugar. Add eggs and vanilla and beat until smooth. Slowly add flour, 1 cup at a time, and finish by stirring in salt. Divide dough into two halves.

✳ Wrap one half in plastic wrap and set aside. Roll out the other half to about ¼-inch thickness and lay tombstone cutouts on top. Cut out the shapes around the patterns using a sharp blade. Place tombstones on prepared baking sheet.

✳ Bake for 8 to 12 minutes, until edges begin to brown.

NOTE: Omitting a leavening agent (baking soda, baking powder) prevents these cookies from changing shape and allows more control when a specific form is desired.

TOMBSTONE GLAZE

1½ cups confectioners' sugar
4 teaspoons whole milk
2 teaspoons light corn syrup
½ teaspoon almond extract
Black food coloring

✳ In a medium bowl, mix the confectioners' sugar, milk, corn syrup, and almond extract. Whisk until smooth, and add just a drop or two of black food coloring to give the mixture a gray color.

✳ Using a small brush, paint the front of each tombstone cookie with glaze; allow to set. Using a blade, carve in whatever lettering you like: RIP, X, dates, or even your friends' initials. Mix a little water with some more black food coloring and lightly brush the dried cookies for a grimy aged appearance.

✳ ASSEMBLY & PRESENTATION

Two (18-ounce) packages Oreos
Modeling Chocolate, in white
    (page 10; optional)
Pumpkin candies (optional)

✳ Tear sections of brownie off of the large sheets and build several hills on a serving tray. Use remaining brownie to create a smooth, yet hilly surface.

✳ Put Oreos in a food processor and grind, 1 handful at a time, until mixture resembles dirt. Coat brownie graveyard with "dirt."

✳ Stand cookies up in the graveyard, using toothpicks behind for support. You can also sculpt skulls and bones out of white modeling chocolate for additional fun, and throw in a few seasonal pumpkin candies as well.

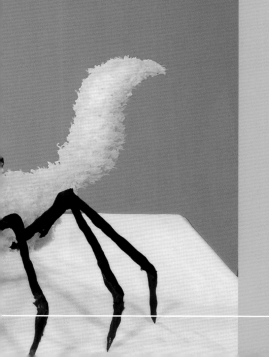

Neapolitan Monster CAKE

Finding a man is pretty easy; keeping him, however, can be a little trickier. After years of unreturned phone calls and restraining orders, I decided I needed a new approach. I started by figuring out what I need most from a man. My conclusion was that it was someone who would listen to me.

The nice thing about this epiphany was that it simplified the parts I'd need—after all, arms and legs are hard to come by, and in the end, they can be used for escape. So I went into my kitchen with the ingredients to create my dream man.

The end result still needs a little work in the attitude department, but the flavor is top-notch, and the fact that you can blame him for any weight you gain is an added bonus!

Neapolitan Monster CAKE

Makes one 12-layer cake

CHOCOLATE CAKE

2 recipes Chocolate Cake, (page 5) baked in one 14-inch, one 10-inch, and four 8-inch round cake pans

STRAWBERRY CAKE

2 cups (4 sticks) unsalted butter, softened, plus more for pans

5 cups cake flour, plus more for pans

4 cups granulated sugar

4 extra-large eggs

2 tablespoons lemon juice

4 teaspoons vanilla extract

½ cup strawberry-flavored gelatin powder, such as Jell-O

1 teaspoon baking soda

½ teaspoon salt

2 cups buttermilk

1⅓ cups chopped fresh strawberries

✳ Preheat oven to 375°F. Butter and flour one 14-inch, one 10-inch, and four 8-inch round cake pans. In a stand mixer, cream together butter and sugar. Add eggs and beat until smooth. Add lemon juice and vanilla and beat until incorporated.

✳ In a separate bowl, combine flour, gelatin, baking soda, and salt. Begin incorporating dry ingredients into wet ingredients, alternating with additions of buttermilk and beat until smooth. Once combined, fold in strawberries. Scoop batter into prepared cake pans.

✳ Bake for 35 to 45 minutes, until a toothpick inserted into centers comes out clean. Do not open oven door before the 30-minute mark. Allow to cool for 10 minutes before removing from baking pans. Promptly wrap in plastic wrap and chill until ready to assemble.

ASSEMBLY & PRESENTATION

Vanilla Buttercream Frosting (page 6), tinted pink plus 2 teaspoons strawberry extract (optional)

Three 10-inch wooden skewers

Hot-glue gun

Modeling Chocolate, in white (page 10)

Modeling Chocolate, in brown (page 10)

Modeling Chocolate, in black (page 10)

Modeling Chocolate, in pink (page 10)

Black fondant

Silver fondant

Edible silver powder

Clear piping gel

✳ Retrieve cakes from fridge and slice each horizontally into two layers. Center one 14-inch strawberry cake layer onto a serving tray. Spread with a generous layer of pink buttercream. Top with 14-inch chocolate cake layer; spread with another layer of buttercream. Place second 14-inch strawberry cake on top, followed by more frosting, and then second 14-inch chocolate cake layer. Repeat for 10-inch strawberry and chocolate layers. Apply crumb coat with more buttercream and then chill for at least 30 minutes until frosting has set. Frost on another layer of pink buttercream and chill once more. Smooth frosting with water-moistened fingertips and then chill until ready to decorate.

✳ For monster head, hot-glue three wooden skewers, in a triangle formation, to an 8-inch base. Stack on 8-inch strawberry and chocolate layers through skewers and onto your base, alternating between cake and buttercream frosting. Chill for at least 30 minutes before continuing.

✳ Using a serrated blade and sculpting tools, create the basic features of the monster—neck (curving in slightly for the chin), eye sockets, nose, brow ridge, and the signature Frankenstein forehead (see photo page 196). Apply crumb coat with buttercream and then chill again for 30 minutes before frosting in final layer. Chill once more until fully set.

✳ Create eyes by rolling white modeling chocolate into two balls roughly 1 inch in diameter. Flatten two pea-size balls of brown modeling chocolate for the irises and smaller balls of black modeling chocolate for the pupils. With pink modeling chocolate, create the ears, nose, eyebrows, and eyelids. Chill until firm.

✳ Adhere all of the modeling chocolate pieces to the cake using a dab of buttercream frosting. Chill until firm. Using a filbert brush, carefully paint a layer of buttercream to cover any seams between

Continued

the modeling chocolate pieces and the rest of the cake. Chill until frosting is fully set and firm. Using sculpting tools, add in the mouth and the creases to the monster's forehead and under eye area. Chill again until firm, and then smooth frosting with water-moistened fingertips.

✳ Roll out black fondant to about ¼-inch thick and cut a rectangle approximately 2 inches by 25 inches for the collar. Cut out 4 to 6 hexagons, each about ½ to ¾ inch in diameter, for the collar, and two hexagons about 1 inch in diameter for the bolts.

✳ Roll a few pea-size balls of black fondant and flatten slightly. Make a horizontal score across the top of each ball (but do not cut all the way through) to create a few screw tops to decorate the collar. With a small dab of buttercream, adhere the screws and the smaller hexagons to the collar.

✳ For the bolts, roll out a log about 2 inches long and ¾ inch in diameter. Cut in half and score in the ridges on each section. Insert a toothpick through each bolt, leaving about ¼ inch exposed at the top to connect the large hexagons, and the remainder at the other end to connect to the cake.

✳ For the chain, roll out 12 logs of fondant, about 3 inches long and ¼ inch in diameter. Create an oval link with the first log and then add each log for the successive links.

✳ After all fondant pieces have set, brush with edible silver powder mixed with 1 tablespoon of vodka. Allow to dry and then chill until ready to attach to cake.

CHOCOLATE GANACHE

1 cup heavy whipping cream
16 ounces chocolate chips
1 teaspoon vanilla extract
1 tablespoon unsalted butter

※ Bring cream to a boil over medium heat in a large saucepan. Reduce heat to low and add chocolate chips. Stir until completely melted and creamy. Turn off heat and add vanilla and butter, stirring quickly to blend evenly.

※ Transfer about half of ganache to a pastry bag fitted with a small round tip. Pipe in the edge of the monster's hairline onto the cake and allow to partially set. Spread reserved ganache over the top and sides of the head, piping where additional precision is needed. Chill cake until ganache is fully set and firm.

※ Retrieve base cake layers, and pipe in the spider web–lace pattern with an extra-small, round tip around the 14-inch and 10-inch tiers. Pipe in the spider onto the monster's forehead. Switch to a decorative tip to pipe trim along bottom edge of each tier.

※ When ready to present and serve, place monster head onto base cake. Attached collar, chain, and bolts to cake, using a dab of buttercream to keep collar and bolts from shifting. Use clear piping gel to create a glossy appearance for the eyes. Finally, add pink buttercream roses (page 13) and a pink fondant bowtie to show the softer side of your beloved monster.

Caramel Popcorn CAT

Companionship is important. I've found, however, that humans can be a bit chatty, which can be tricky if you want to ensure your secrets and science experiments are safe. Which is why a friend in the feline family makes an ideal soul mate.

Cats, after all, never gossip; and, considering some of the villainy they're capable of, they tend not to judge so much.

Their only drawback is their shorter life expectancy. So when one of your furry best friends tries to escape this realm through means of a busy highway, I've got a backup plan for you!

With some bolts, borrowed parts, and a lot of voltage, you need never say goodbye again.

Caramel
POPCORN CAT

CARAMEL POPCORN

Makes about 12 cups

2 tablespoons vegetable oil
⅓ cup unpopped popcorn
2 teaspoons coarse salt
½ cup (1 stick) unsalted butter
1 cup packed light brown sugar
½ cup light corn syrup
⅔ cup sweetened condensed milk
½ teaspoon vanilla extract
Melting chocolate, melted, as needed

✳ Place oil and popcorn kernels in a large pot with secure lid. Heat popcorn on stove over medium heat. Once you hear the last kernels popping, turn off heat. Remove lid momentarily to add salt and then close and fasten lid to keep warm.

✳ In a medium saucepan over medium heat, combine butter, brown sugar, corn syrup, and condensed milk. Stirring frequently and using a candy thermometer on the side, heat until mixture reaches 238°F. Immediately remove from heat and stir in vanilla, then immediately pour over warmed popcorn and mix vigorously until evenly coated. (It's hot, so watch out!)

✳ Once cooled enough to handle, create a general cat form: a rounded ball for the head, an elongated oval for the body, and a tail. Molding popcorn all in one piece is best for stability, but separate pieces can be glued together with melting chocolate if necessary. Allow popcorn to cool while making the legs (below).

CHOCOLATE PRETZEL SPIDER LEGS

1 (10-ounce) package 6–7-inch pretzel rods (you won't need this many, but breakage can happen)
Toothpicks
About 20 prepackaged caramels, wrappers removed
1 (10-ounce) package pretzel sticks (you won't need this many, but breakage can happen)
Melting chocolate

✳ Snip eight pretzels rods at the two-thirds mark to create eight short pieces and eight longer pieces. Insert a toothpick into one end of each shorter rod. Warm one caramel with hands and use it to adhere each longer rod piece to a shorter piece (opposite end of the toothpick). Using another warmed caramel, adhere one pretzel stick to the end of each longer rod. Snip the end off two pretzel sticks and insert a toothpick in each. Using a warmed caramel, adhere another pretzel stick to the opposite end. Once all eight legs and two pincers are formed, chill for 30 minutes.

✳ Melt chocolate and line a baking sheet with parchment paper. Dip chilled legs into chocolate and place on parchment paper. Chill for about a half hour until fully set.

1 (7-ounce) jar marshmallow fluff
1 (8-ounce) bag sweetened shredded
    coconut
Modeling Chocolate (page 10)
Edible wafer paper

✳ Prop front and sides of popcorn cat form up on toothpicks to ensure stability and place on a serving tray. Then stick legs and pincers into popcorn ball via exposed toothpicks. Adjust leg positions as necessary to allow your kitty to stand up on its own.

✳ Fill a piping bag with marshmallow fluff and, using a fine round tip, pipe fur all over popcorn. Make eyes, nose, and ears out of modeling chocolate and place accordingly; pipe around each with more fluff. Finish by coating fur with shredded coconut. Snip whiskers out of edible wafer paper and carefully place on face, adhering with a dab of marshmallow fluff.

The Big Bad

BUTTERSCOTCH CAKE

Innocent women being stalked and victimized is a tale as old as time. A perfect example of this is the classic story of Red Riding Hood and her hairy assailant. Whenever I've heard stories like this, I tend to picture myself in the heroine's shoes. With this story in particular, I was always plagued by the thought, "What the heck is she doing wandering through the woods without a gun?" In the original story, she's dependent on the huntsman to save her. In my version, Red's a little more self-sufficient and decides to pack some heat.

Once her adversary has his chance to pounce, she surprises him with her Little Red Rifle and sends him to that Big Bad Boneyard in the Sky.

The Big Bad
BUTTERSCOTCH CAKE

Makes one 4-layer cake

BUTTERSCOTCH CAKE

Softened unsalted butter for pans

3¾ cups all-purpose flour, plus more
for pans

1 tablespoon baking powder

2¼ cups packed light brown sugar

1 teaspoon salt

2¼ cups half-and-half or whole milk

1 cup vegetable oil

1 tablespoon vanilla extract

3 egg whites

½ cup granulated sugar

2 cups butterscotch chips

✳ Preheat oven 350°F. Butter and flour one 10-inch, two 8-inch, and one 5-inch round cake pans. In a medium bowl, mix flour, baking powder, brown sugar, and salt. Add in half-and-half, oil, and vanilla and whisk until smooth.

✳ In a stand mixer, beat egg whites on high speed until stiff peaks form. Pour in granulated sugar and beat on high speed until glossy peaks form. Gently fold into batter and blend with whisk until smooth.

✳ Pour batter into prepared baking pans. Sprinkle butterscotch chips over top. Use a spatula or fork to gently submerge chips. Bake for 25 to 35 minutes, until a toothpick inserted into centers comes out clean. Remove cakes from oven and allow to cool for 10 minutes before removing from pans onto racks. Wrap in plastic wrap and chill until ready to assemble.

BUTTERSCOTCH FROSTING

½ cup (1 stick) unsalted butter

¾ cup packed dark brown sugar

½ cup heavy whipping cream

1 teaspoon vanilla extract

3 cups confectioners' sugar

✳ Melt butter in a medium saucepan. Mix in brown sugar and heat over medium heat, stirring until smooth and creamy. Continue to stir just until mixture bubbles. Add in cream and stir vigorously for about 2 minutes. Remove from heat, add vanilla, and beat until well blended. Allow to cool for 10 minutes. Transfer to a stand mixer and beat in confectioners' sugar, 1 cup at a time, until stiff peaks form.

✳ ASSEMBLY & PRESENTATION

2 cups sweetened coconut flakes

Cocoa powder

Modeling Chocolate, in white
(page 10)

Modeling Chocolate, in brown
(page 10)

Chocolate Buttercream Frosting
(page 7)

1 cup melting chocolate, melted

Corn syrup

Clear piping gel

✳ For this project, I handcrafted a panel of wood, carving in dec-orations and attaching a picture-hanging fixture onto the back. Then I drilled and hot-glued three wooden spikes for stability in the front. I then cleaned it with warm water and painted a mix-ture of cocoa powder and water over it to give it a rustic look and ensure all cracks were filled. If you're not planning on displaying your cake vertically, any serving tray will do.

✳ Retrieve your cakes from fridge. Slice each cake horizon-tally into two layers. Center one 10-inch layer on serving tray or panel. Spread a generous dollop of butterscotch frosting on top and add second 10-inch layer. Continue layering cake and frosting, building up the wolf's head using progressively smaller layers. To create a realistic face and snout, trim middle and top layers with a serrated blade. Once all layers are stacked, use the blade to carve and refine the shape. Use some of the cake scraps to create the ears.

✳ Coat final form evenly with the remaining butterscotch frosting for base crumb coat and then refrigerate for 30 minutes.

✳ In the meantime, preheat oven to 400°F. Toast coconut flakes on a rimmed baking sheet for about 5 minutes. Remove and toss in cocoa powder. Sculpt eyes and teeth out of white modeling chocolate.

✳ Remove cake from fridge and frost on a layer of chocolate buttercream to give definition to wolf head. Carve out two small almond shapes for eyes using a small, sharp blade. Smooth out frosting using water-moistened fingertips. Add a little base texture by taking a fork and carving grooves in the direction of where fur would grow. Chill for another 30 minutes.

✳ Glue in eyes and teeth using melting chocolate. Once set, begin applying coconut hair by lightly basting exterior of cake with corn syrup, section by section, and then sprinkling coconut over syrup. (I went in afterward and individually glued in long shards of coconut to give a direction to the hair growth.) Eyes were coated last with prepackaged clear piping gel to give a wet appearance.

✳ After chilling overnight, my cake was ready to be hung and photographed. While the cake is cold it will remain supported on your secured wooden spikes. However, don't leave it hanging for long, as the frosting softens to room temperature and will become unsecured. But for a little while, this cake makes quite a statement and is seriously delicious!

Terror MISU

Cellar doors, trap doors, and secret passageways. Who doesn't love them? They instantly add an air of mystery and intrigue to any dwelling. Every eerie movie or television show I watched growing up had one. They are the places you hide your secrets and escape to when in danger. So why in god's name are they not in every house that's built? I suppose that's a question for another time, but the point I'm making here is that any house of mine will always have all three! Where else am I supposed to store my home-made preserves, liquor, and lycanthropes?

Living in Twin Peaks has some wonderful bene-fits, but one of the big drawbacks I've found is a ter-rible werewolf infestation. Luckily, they're generally not the brightest, which makes them easy to trap. A few months back, I caught one not much bigger than myself and decided to keep it. You never know when a recipe or potion is going to call for the whisker of a wolf-man, and I like to keep my supplies as fresh as possible. This one in particular happens to be rather docile and has grown quite fond of my treats. So I decided to bake it something special.

Terror–MISU

Makes 12 servings

LADY FINGERS

Makes about 20 lady fingers

6 eggs, separated
3 tablespoons granulated sugar
1½ cups all-purpose flour
1 teaspoon baking powder

✳ Preheat oven to 400°F. Line several baking sheets with parchment paper. In a stand mixer, whip egg whites on high speed until frothy. Add sugar and beat until stiff and glossy peaks form. In a second bowl, whisk egg yolks until light in color. In a third bowl, combine flour and baking powder. Gently fold half the egg whites into the beaten yolks. Slowly fold flour mixture into yolks, then finish by mixing in remaining egg whites. Gently fold everything together and transfer to a pastry bag.

✳ Pipe about twenty 3-inch-long strips on prepared baking sheets using a large round tip. Use remaining batter to create two 8-inch spiral disks on prepared baking sheets. (The same diameter of your cake mold.) Bake each sheet for 8 to 10 minutes, until just beginning to brown. Remove from oven and allow to cool to room temperature. (Note: If any of the fingers or disks is too long, you can snip it with shears, as they won't be showing in the final cake.)

TIRAMISU FILLING

6 egg yolks
¾ cup granulated sugar
⅔ cup whole milk
2 cups mascarpone cheese
1½ cups heavy whipping cream
1 tablespoon cornstarch
1 teaspoon vanilla extract

✳ Whisk together egg yolks and sugar in a medium saucepan. Beat in milk and heat over medium heat until boiling, stirring constantly. Reduce heat and stir for another minute. Then remove from heat and transfer to a heatproof bowl; refrigerate until chilled, about 1½ hours.

✳ In a stand mixer, beat cold egg mixture with mascarpone cheese until light and fluffy. Scoop back into bowl, and place back in fridge to chill.

✳ Beat cream in a clean stand mixer; add cornstarch and vanilla and beat on high speed until stiff peaks form. Cover and place in fridge.

½ cup strong coffee

1 tablespoon Kahlúa

1 tablespoon rum

½ cup cocoa powder

Sugar Cookie dough (page 82)

10 almonds

White melting chocolate, melted

Chocolate Buttercream Frosting
  (page 7)

Vanilla Buttercream Frosting
  (page 6)

10 chocolate-covered coffee beans

✳ Mix coffee, Kahlúa, and rum in a small bowl. Brush over one side of lady fingers and disks.

✳ Line an 8-inch wide and 5-inch deep cake mold with high sides with parchment paper. Line sides tightly with lady fingers (this is a bit tricky). In the center, layer a third of the whipped cream mixture, followed with half of the custard, and then topped with the first lady finger disk; add another layer of whipped cream, custard, and a disk. Cover with plastic wrap and refrigerate for 8 hours.

✳ Invert tiramisu on a cake stand and remove the parchment paper. Coat entire tiramisu with remaining whipped cream and a layer of cocoa powder. Set in fridge until ready to decorate.

✳ Preheat oven to 375°F. Mold firm sugar cookie dough into ten fingerlike shapes. Create a shaping support beam out of aluminum foil to rest and bake your fingers/claws on. Press an almond into the tip of each finger to create a divot for a fingernail (remove almond). Bake for 8 to 12 minutes, until just beginning to brown. Remove from oven and allow to cool to room temperature.

✳ Use melted white chocolate to adhere a chocolate-coated almond fingernail into the divot made previously. Remove tiramisu from fridge and place claws around edge. If they aren't sticking, glue them with a bit of chocolate buttercream. Pipe the spaces between claws on the sides of the cake with chocolate buttercream using a decorative nozzle. Pipe spider webs artistically here and there using white buttercream, and make little spiders by placing a chocolate-covered coffee bean in center and piping chocolate buttercream legs.

Vampire MILKSHAKE

Immortality is a notion that has always appealed to me. Given folklore throughout the centuries, I'm inclined to believe I'm not alone in this sentiment. We are born into this world without being asked and are initially endowed with youth, beauty, and vigor. However, as the years pass, all of those things begin to dim and tarnish . . . but what if they didn't?

Myths about vampires are nearly as old as mankind, and have enthralled me ever since I was first introduced to the tales. These dark, mysterious creatures were beautiful, strong, and everlasting—with only one big caveat: they needed blood to survive.

This was the one thing about them that had always bothered me. Not that they have to kill people, not that they couldn't ever bask in the sunlight—but that the only thing they get to consume for the rest of time tastes like dirty pennies!

I could get used to killing people; let's face it: there are a lot of you. And I have never been one to lie around in the sun. But no more ice cream? This was unacceptable. I had to come up with a solution.

So a few hundred years ago, I did some experimenting, and discovered it isn't blood that satiates vampires; it's just the color red. It's a shame so many people had to die over such a silly oversight . . . but as they say, hindsight is 20/20.

With the passage of time, incredible things have been invented, but none so great as red dye #40. This miraculous liquid pigment has opened up a bevy of menu options to the undead, and the following recipe is of my longtime favorites.

Vampire
MILKSHAKE

6 cups (3 pints) chocolate ice cream
1 tablespoon vanilla extract
¼ cup granulated sugar
2 ounces bourbon
2½ cups whole milk
2 bottles red food coloring

ADDITIONAL
1 cup blood-red melting chocolate
4 vintage shake glasses
Whipped cream
Straws

✳ Melt red melting chocolate in a medium saucepan. Dip rim of glasses in melted chocolate; set upright to set. Pour remaining chocolate into a piping bag and pipe around the rim, allowing it to overflow in ominous drips.

✳ In a blender, combine half of remaining ingredients—ice cream, vanilla, sugar, bourbon, milk, and red food coloring—and blend. Divide shake between two glasses and set in freezer. Repeat with remaining ingredients. Set out all four glasses and top with whipped cream and straws.

Devil's Food CAKE

It's said that the devil comes in many disguises. He's been known to take the form of a snake, the actor Al Pacino, or—his most fearsome guise—the IRS agent. He often comes making promises with hidden agendas. Maybe you want to be thinner, richer, or live forever? The bottom line is, if you're considering signing a contract with him, it would behoove you to read the fine print.

This next recipe is no exception. As I began baking it, I discovered there's a good reason that it has earned the moniker "devil's food cake." It's so moist, creamy, and delicious, you can't help but overindulge. If you don't believe me, just make the frosting and, before it's set, lick the back of the spoon . . . and you will instantly understand what I'm talking about.

For the exterior on this one, I was inspired by some of the artwork done for Francis Ford Coppola's masterpiece *Dracula*. While the method I use is complicated and time-consuming, I'd say my efforts are well worth the trouble. As the saying goes, the devil is in the details.

Devil's Food
CAKE

Makes four 10-inch square cakes

3 cups (6 sticks) unsalted butter, softened, plus more for pans

4 cups all-purpose flour, plus more for pans

4 cups granulated sugar

2 tablespoons vanilla extract

6 extra-large eggs, room temperature

2½ cups water

½ cup whole milk

1½ cups cocoa powder

2 teaspoons baking soda

2 teaspoons baking powder

2 teaspoons salt

✳ Preheat oven to 350°F. Butter and flour four 10-inch square cake pans. In a stand mixer, cream together butter and sugar on medium-high speed until light and airy. Add vanilla and eggs, one at a time, and beat until creamy and smooth.

✳ In a medium saucepan, combine water and milk and bring to a boil, stirring frequently. In a separate bowl combine flour, cocoa powder, baking soda, baking powder, and salt. Add flour and milk mixtures to batter on low speed, alternating in small portions, and beat until just combined; do not overbeat.

✳ Divide batter among prepared pans. Bake for 25 to 35 minutes, until a toothpick inserted into centers comes out clean. Allow to cool for 10 minutes before removing from pans, then wrap in plastic and refrigerate pieces until ready to assemble.

CHOCOLATE GANACHE FROSTING

22 ounces chocolate chips, finely chopped

2 cups heavy whipping cream

✳ Place chocolate chips in a large heatproof bowl. Heat cream in a medium saucepan until it boils, stirring constantly. Pour hot cream over chocolate, making sure to fully saturate; allow to sit for 5 minutes. Whisk together by hand until very smooth and blended. Cover with plastic wrap and allow to rest for 1½ hours. Once set, it can be spread or piped like buttercream frosting.

Shredded wheat
Oreos
Dark brown sugar

✳ Retrieve cakes from fridge and slice each horizontally into two layers. Cut in half from top to bottom to create a total of sixteen rectangular layers. Center one layer on serving dish and spread with a generous dollop of frosting; continue stacking, alternating between cake and frosting. For added stability, insert one or two wooden stakes vertically through stacked cake. Round the top like a headstone using a serrated blade. Apply a crumb coat on entire cake using chocolate ganache frosting. Allow cake to chill until frosting is fully set, and then smooth with water-moistened fingertips, if necessary. Allow cake to set once more before piping decorative details with remaining frosting.

✳ I used sculpting tools from a cake supply store to create the devil, but you could easily pipe a name or initials instead. For an authentic-looking grave, put Oreos, brown sugar, and shredded wheat in a food processor and chop till earthy-looking. Surround base of cake with this mixture, and no one will know it isn't real earth and twigs!

Tarantula
COOKIES

It's strange to me that tarantulas are so feared. After all, they're not exactly the pit bull of the spider world. For the most part, they spend their time meandering about passively. I think it's the fact that they look like the epitome of evil that sets people on edge.

Much like the characters in the 1960s television program *The Munsters*, I consider tarantulas a perfect medley of sinister comedy and eerie beauty. In honor of one of the best shows ever made and my very favorite spider, I've made a deliciously sweet snack in their likeness—which will hopefully make you laugh while also filling you up on a healthy dose of nightmare fuel.

Tarantula COOKIES

Makes 10 to 12 tarantulas

1¼ cups (2½ sticks) unsalted butter, softened, plus more for pans

3½ cups all-purpose flour, plus more for pans

1 cup granulated sugar

1 teaspoon pure vanilla extract

1 teaspoon salt

✳ Preheat oven to 375°F. Butter and flour two baking sheets. Cream together butter and sugar in a stand mixer. Add vanilla, salt, and flour and beat until dough forms. Wrap in plastic wrap and chill for 1 hour.

✳ Using clean hands, shape dough into bodies and legs. First, divide dough into ten to twelve roughly equal parts. Use each part to create: an approximately ½-inch round ball, a flattened oval with four indentations on each side, eight legs approximately 1 to 2 inches long and bent into a V shape, and two small pincers. Arrange bodies on one baking sheet and legs on the other. Bake cookies for 7 to 15 minutes, until edges are just beginning to brown.

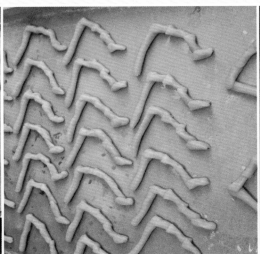

Homemade Caramel (page 7) or
    Royal Icing (page 9)
2 cups dark melting chocolate, melted
1 cup shredded sweetened coconut,
    toasted

✳ Depending on your comfort level, you can either use caramel or royal icing to adhere legs to each body. If using caramel, work quickly to adhere legs by dipping joints in caramel and attaching to body. But be careful! The caramel is very hot and will set quickly.

✳ If you're feeling like you'd rather take it a little slower, use royal icing as glue and allow each leg to fully set before adhering the next.

✳ Once spiders are formed, coat entirely with dark melting chocolate and pipe eyes and fangs. Finish by sprinkling toasted coconut over backs.

Winter

Serpentine CINNAMON ROLLS

Life is filled with some pretty amazing things. As cultures come together, they share with the world the best of their homeland. Mexico gave us the taco, Japan gave us sushi, and Sweden brought us *kanelbullar*—better known in the States as cinnamon rolls. They're the perfect mix of a buttery, flakey crust; gooey icing; and comforting cinnamon flavor.

But I've found cinnamon rolls are like people: 99 percent of them are incredibly wonderful, and a small percentage have a bad attitude. Such is the case with the tasty little serpents to follow. They may be made of the most delicious stuff on Earth, but that won't stop them from biting you right back.

Serpentine
CINNAMON ROLLS

Makes 1 dozen snakes

DOUGH

¼ cup water

¼ cup whole milk

1 tablespoon yeast

¼ cup (½ stick) unsalted butter, softened, plus more for bowl and pans

2 cups all-purpose flour, plus more for dusting

½ teaspoon salt

1 teaspoon ground cinnamon

¼ cup granulated sugar

✳ In a stand mixer using a dough hook, mix water, milk, yeast, butter, flour, salt, cinnamon, and sugar. Once dough ball forms, remove from mixer and place in a large greased bowl. Allow to rise, covered with a dish towel (do not let it sit directly on the dough), for 1 hour.

FILLING

3½ tablespoons unsalted butter, softened, plus more for pans

All-purpose flour for pans

¼ cup granulated sugar

1 teaspoon ground cinnamon

¼ teaspoon ground nutmeg

✳ Preheat oven to 425°F. Butter and flour two rimmed baking sheets.

✳ In a small bowl, mix butter, sugar, cinnamon, and nutmeg with a rubber spatula until a paste forms.

✳ Roll dough ball on a floured surface into a large rectangle about ⅛ inch thick. Spread filling over one half of the dough. Fold other half over filling and press together very lightly. Use a pastry cutter to slice dough vertically into 1-inch-wide strips. Cut across each strip lengthwise to divide into three-fourths and one-fourth parts to create tails and heads.

✳ For the tails, twist each long piece gently (like a candy cane) and then coil into snakelike figures on prepared baking sheet. Leave a slight opening at the center of your coil, where you will later insert heads.

✳ For the heads, flatten short pieces into ovals with a little tail at the end, like a spoon with the handle mostly cut off. Make a foil mold that to create a rolling S shape; place on baking sheet and dust with flour; and place snake heads on mold as pictured on page 233.

EGG WASH

1 extra-large egg, beaten

¼ cup water

1 teaspoon salt

✳ In a small bowl, whisk egg, water, and salt together. Using a pastry brush, baste heads and tails with egg wash. Bake for 9 to 12 minutes, until lightest areas are a golden brown. Remove from oven and allow to cool to room temperature before assembling and decorating.

✳ ASSEMBLY & PRESENTATION

CINNAMON ICING

1 egg white

1½ cups confectioners' sugar

2 teaspoons ground cinnamon

1 teaspoon ground cloves

Brown food coloring

Royal Icing (page 9; optional)

✳ In a stand mixer, beat egg white, confectioners' sugar, cinnamon, cloves, and brown food coloring to desired shade in a stand mixer until smooth. Scoop into a pastry bag with a small round tip.

✳ Pipe a small amount of icing around each opening in the coils. Gently insert heads into each opening. If necks are too long, carefully trim with a sharp blade. To stabilize, pipe around each neck once more, if necessary.

✳ Pipe icing diagonally across snake bodies to accentuate coils and around edges of heads.

WHITE ICING

You can use royal icing for sharp details like the eyes and tongues, or use the following icing for something slightly messier and more delicious.

2 cups confectioners' sugar

3 tablespoons heavy whipping cream

1 teaspoon vanilla extract

½ teaspoon salt

✳ In a bowl, whisk together confectioners' sugar, cream, vanilla, and salt by hand. Pour over buns for a gooey glaze or dust with confectioners' sugar.

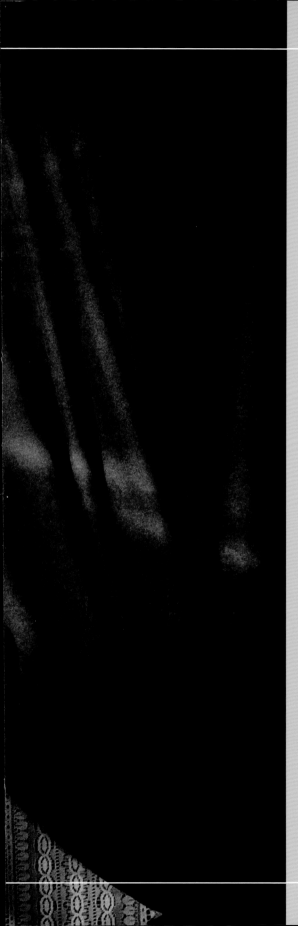

Black and White CAKE

Buildings and structures have always fascinated me, and I think it's because for me, figuring out how things are constructed is fun. Shapes, lighting, and angles are very interesting and eye-catching.

Getting creative with cakes is a perfect way to improve your skills and understanding of how things are built. The wonderful thing about working with such a sweet medium is that if you mess up, it's typically pretty easy to correct. This project, for instance, was done for a friend's birthday, and it gave me a chance to experiment with a new flavor and a unique shape.

It's not exactly the Mona Lisa, but it is fun to look at and tastes amazing. I use prepackaged rice pudding throughout the layers, which adds a mellow and light texture to the whole cake.

Black and White CAKE

Makes one 3-layer cake

MOCHA CAKE

Softened unsalted butter for pans

1¾ cups all-purpose flour, plus more
    for pans

2 cups granulated sugar

¾ cup cocoa powder

1½ teaspoons baking soda

1½ teaspoons baking powder

2 teaspoons salt

1 cup buttermilk

½ cup vegetable oil

2 extra-large eggs

2 teaspoons vanilla extract

1 cup very hot coffee

✳ Preheat oven to 350°F. Butter and flour one 10-inch square, one 8-inch square, and one 5-inch square baking pan. In a large bowl, whisk together flour, sugar, cocoa powder, baking soda, baking powder, salt, buttermilk, oil, eggs, and vanilla. Mix until roughly blended. Add piping hot coffee last and mix quickly. Divide among prepared pans.

✳ Bake for 35 to 45 minutes, until a toothpick inserted into centers comes out clean. Allow to cool for 10 minutes before removing from pans. Promptly wrap in plastic wrap and chill until ready to assemble.

WHITE CAKE

1 cup (2 sticks) unsalted butter,
    softened, plus more for pans

3 cups all-purpose flour, plus more
    for pans

1½ cups granulated sugar

4 large eggs, room temperature

1 tablespoon vanilla extract

¾ cup heavy whipping cream

1 tablespoon baking powder

½ teaspoon salt

✳ Preheat oven to 375°F. Butter and flour one 10-inch square, one 8-inch square, and one 5-inch square baking pan. In a stand mixer, cream together butter and sugar until fluffy. Add one egg at a time, beating between additions. In a separate bowl, combine vanilla and cream. In a third bowl, whisk together flour, baking powder, and salt. Add flour and cream mixtures to batter in mixer on low speed, alternating between the two until fully combined. Divide among prepared baking dishes.

✳ Bake for 25 to 35 minutes, until a toothpick inserted into centers comes out clean. Allow to cool for 10 minutes before removing from pans. Promptly wrap in plastic wrap and chill until ready to assemble.

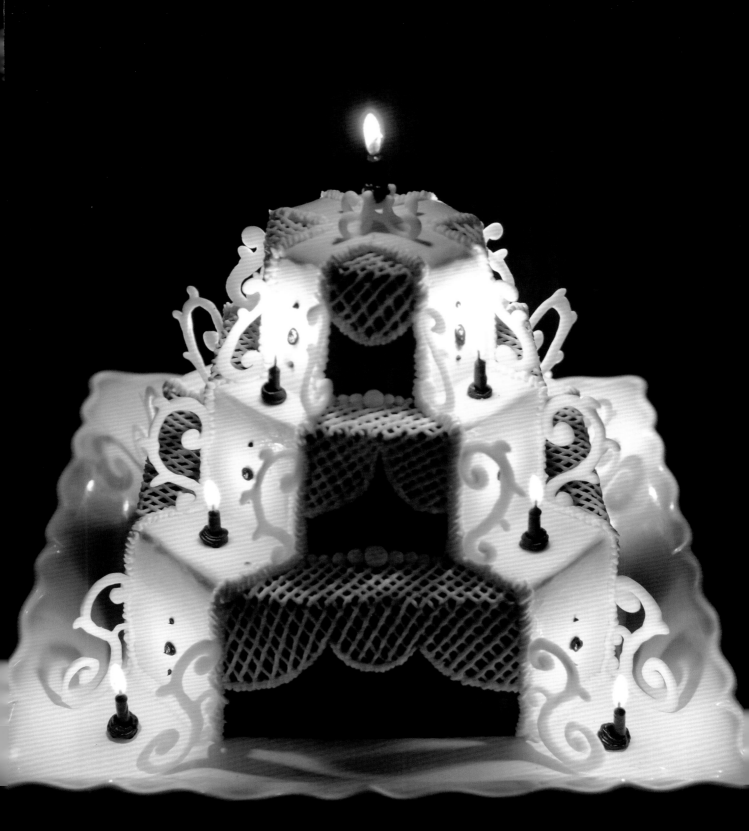

※ ※ ASSEMBLY & PRESENTATION

Chocolate Buttercream Frosting
(page 7)
Black food coloring
Cake board, cut into one 10-inch diameter octagon, one 8-inch diameter octagon, and one 5-inch diameter octagon
Vanilla Buttercream Frosting
(page 6)
Two 22-ounce tubs rice pudding
Semisweet chocolate chips
White melting chocolate

※ Tint half of chocolate buttercream with black food coloring; set aside.

※ Retrieve cakes from fridge. Use cake boards as a guide to trim the edges of each cake to form an octagon. Slice each cake horizontally to create two layers each.

※ Place 10-inch cake board on a serving tray, followed by one 10-inch white cake layer. Spread over a generous layer of vanilla buttercream. Top with a 10-inch mocha cake layer. Spread over a generous layer of chocolate buttercream. Top with another 10-inch white cake layer. Spread over a generous layer of rice pudding and sprinkle with a small handful of chocolate chips. Top with second 10-inch mocha cake layer.

※ Spread a thin layer of chocolate buttercream in a roughly 8-inch circle on top center of cake. Place 8-inch cake board on top and repeat layering process for 8-inch and 5-inch cake sections.

※ Apply crumb coat with remaining chocolate buttercream. Chill cake until fully set, then frost in a layer of black buttercream, keeping edges as smooth and straight as possible. Chill once more, then smooth frosting with water-moistened fingertips. If necessary, chill once more before proceeding.

※ Using a small round tip, pipe an outline in vanilla buttercream for your white sections. Once set, fill in with vanilla buttercream, keeping edges as smooth and straight as possible. Chill until set and then smooth frosting with water-moistened fingertips.

※ While cake is chilling, sketch outlines for your decorative scrolls onto a piece of parchment paper. You will need at least twenty-four, plus the top decoration, but I suggest creating a few more in case of breakage. Place parchment paper on a cookie sheet. Melt the white melting chocolate gently in a heavy-bottomed pan. Carefully transfer melted chocolate to a pastry bag with small round tip. Pipe chocolate along patterns and then chill until fully set.

✳ Once cake has chilled, pipe in additional decoration onto black sections with white buttercream using a fine round tip. Switch to a more decorative tip and pipe along edges of white sections. Before edges have fully set, carefully place white chocolate scrolls around each tier. If desired, pipe small circular details onto center of each white section with black buttercream.

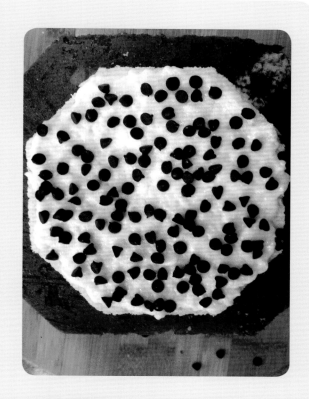

Hansel and Gretel

GINGERBREAD CASTLE

To be honest, not all fairy tales make a whole lot of sense. The story of Hansel and Gretel, for instance, has always baffled me. Let's say you had the magical ability to create an edible house made of all your favorite desserts—then why would you have any interest in eating children? They're noisy, they smell, and they're very difficult to catch.

This brings me to another hole in the plot: If you were trying to wrangle children for a stew, why would you hype them up on sugar first? Wouldn't a house with a jungle gym be more logical? Anyhow, I consider myself a good sport, and am willing to embrace the character whether or not I understand her motives, mainly because I just wanted to build another edible house.

Creating a gingerbread house is a timeless holiday tradition, and a wonderful way to spend time arguing with your family. This year, I challenge you to leave the premade kits at the store—and create something vastly more expensive and time-consuming!

Hansel and Gretel GINGERBREAD CASTLE

Makes 1 gingerbread castle

GINGERBREAD

2 cups (4 sticks) unsalted butter, softened

2 cups packed dark brown sugar

1½ cups light molasses

¼ cup ground cinnamon

¼ cup ground ginger

4 teaspoons ground cloves

4 teaspoons ground nutmeg

8 cups all-purpose flour

½ cup water

ADDITIONAL

Card stock

✳ In a stand mixer, cream together butter, brown sugar, molasses, and spices. Blend in flour and water. Mix until a dough just forms. Separate dough into three equal balls, wrap in plastic, and refrigerate for at least 1 hour.

✳ While dough is chilling, measure, draw, and cut templates for your gingerbread house out of card stock or very thick paper. I encourage you to dream up your own structure—a castle, your childhood home, a small cottage—but in any case you will need: four rectangles for the walls (with windows and doors cut out), two rectangles for the roof, and two triangles to fill the space between your walls and the roof. (In my case, I opted to leave the back side of my castle open, so that I could add in the Hansel and Gretel figurines and small battery-operated flicker lights at the end.) If you decide to create your own design, it takes some math and problem-solving, so make sure to sketch out an idea of what you want to make and have a ruler handy to ensure your pieces will fit together smoothly. Label each template and mark how many of each shape you will need to cut out.

✳ Preheat oven to 400°F. Retrieve first dough ball from fridge and roll out to about ⅛-inch thickness on a floured surface. Lay card-stock templates down (as many as will fit) and, using an X-Acto knife or other sharp blade, cut out shapes and place on a cookie sheet. Combine dough scraps and roll out to ⅛-inch thickness again. Repeat with remaining dough until all shapes have been cut out.

✳ Bake gingerbread for 12 to 15 minutes, until edges begin to darken. Make sure not to under bake, as you want your pieces stiff and rigid. Remove from oven and allow to cool to room temperature before assembly.

CANDY CANE TRIM

1 cup water
1 cup granulated sugar
1 cup light corn syrup
½ teaspoon cream of tartar
½ teaspoon peppermint extract
Red food coloring

✳ Combine water, sugar, corn syrup, and cream of tartar in a deep heavy-bottomed pot. Mix until dissolved, then clip a candy thermometer on side of pot; heat over medium-low heat *without stirring* until the temperature reads 280°F (soft-crack stage). Heating too quickly will cause a yellowish discoloration, so be very patient. Remove from heat and gently stir in peppermint extract. Once mixed, pour half of the mixture into a smaller pot and the remaining onto a silicone mat. Put a drop or two of red food coloring into mixture in the pot (to achieve pink) and leave on stove where it can remain warm without cooking any further.

✳ Once mixture on silicone mat cools enough to touch, start kneading it by pulling, folding, and blending back into itself. Do this until mixture is pure white. Wrap in silicone mat and place back on stove where it will be warm but won't cook.

✳ Pour pink mixture onto another silicon mat and knead it until a glossy and opaque ball. Retrieve white candy ball. Divide each ball into four equal parts and roll out each into long ropes about 12 inches in length. Cut each rope in half. Stack two white and two pink ropes, alternating colors. Repeat for remaining ropes. Roll each stack together and lengthen until desired width is reached, twisting as you go to create the candy cane effect. (I stopped rolling when ropes were about ⅛ inch in thickness.) Quickly measure, shape, and cut each candy cane window trim, using cookie templates as a guide. Extra candy can be shaped into spirals and traditional canes for additional decorations.

✳ This is a good method to creating a customized and delicious trim, but you can also take the safer route and use store-bought canes or make them out of fondant if children are involved in the process.

✳ ✳ ASSEMBLY & PRESENTATION

Candy Glass (page 42)
Royal Icing (page 9)
Brown food coloring
Fondant (page 11), mixed with
    ½ cup cocoa powder
Cotton candy
Red food coloring
Modeling Chocolate, in beige-yellow
    (page 10)
Edible paint

ADDITIONAL
X-Acto knife
Ruler

✳ For the windows, use a very sharp blade and a ruler as a guide to score candy glass into the size and shape needed to fit windows. Once glass shapes have been scored several times, it will easily break into desired shapes. Attach windows to the back side of gingerbread walls using a bit of royal icing around the edges. Allow to set for at least 5 minutes.

✳ Once windows have been added, adhere gingerbread walls together using a little royal icing that you tinted brown, piped along the connecting edge of each piece. Allow each piece to set and dry for at least 5 minutes before moving on. Next, adhere the triangles to the top edge of two opposite walls and hold in place until fully set. Finally, adhere the two rectangles to create the roof. With more brown royal icing, pipe in window and door panes using a fine round tip. Allow to fully set and harden.

✳ For the roof tiles, roll out brown fondant into a rectangle about ⅛-inch thick. Using a ruler and an X-Acto knife or other sharp blade, trim each side to create straight edges. Cut rectangle into horizontal strips about an inch wide. Then cut vertically about

every ½ inch, creating small rectangles about 1 inch x ½ inch. On each rectangle, trim two corners off one end as shown.

✳ Starting with the bottom row and working up, add in the roof tiles, adhering with remaining brown royal icing. Lightly brush with water for a shiny appearance.

✳ With a small round tip, pipe royal icing around edges of each window and adhere candy cane trim. Allow to fully set. Pipe in additional decoration around outer edges of each window with more white royal icing.

✳ For the snowy lawn and roof, switch to a thicker decorative tip and pipe in a complete border with white royal icing. In a separate small bowl, mix more royal icing with 3 tablespoons water. Carefully pour a small amount of the watered-down icing into your border, until the surface is completely covered, and allow to fully set.

✳ Add in small tufts of cotton candy, rolled slightly into loose balls to create bushes. Pipe additional decorative details onto house and yard with royal icing tinted pink.

✳ Sculpt the basic shapes of the unfortunate Hansel and Gretel out of beige-yellow modeling chocolate. Pierce each body about halfway with thin wooden skewers—this will allow better control over rotating the bodies while decorating. Refine the shape of the figurines. Using edible paints, add in facial features and pink skin tones. Pipe in clothing with white (Gretel) and brown (Hansel) royal icing. Allow figurines to completely set and then remove skewers. Add the children to the house by adhering with more royal icing.

NOTE: If you've left the back side of your gingerbread house open, you can also add small battery-operated flicker lights for added effect.

Reddit
CAKE

As the people on this planet evolve, some truly amazing things happen, and it's usually the things you hardly notice that ultimately result in the biggest changes. The invention of the Internet is the single most amazing thing that has come about in my lifetime. In so many ways, it has brought us all together and made knowledge accessible to so many people.

Reddit is an entertainment and social-media site that was created in 2005 with a simple platform: People post things and other people either vote it up or vote it down, and you can also comment. This concept became so popular that the site now has millions of viewers from all over the globe. This new form of social democracy is why you're reading this book. Without sites like Reddit, it's doubtful that any of my work would have seen the light of day, so obviously I'm grateful.

But like most things that are wonderful, there is always a dark side. The anonymity of the Internet has given way to Internet trolling, an outlet for frustrated people to wage their battles and grievances online, without consequences. Sites like Reddit have shown me that, while the majority of people are kind and good-hearted, we are still living amongst pitchfork-wielding heathens. This cake is my homage to such individuals.

Reddit CAKE

Makes one 4-layer cake

CHOCOLATE CAKE

Softened unsalted butter for pans

3½ cups all-purpose flour, plus more
    for pans

2 cups boiling water

4 cups granulated sugar

1½ cups Dutch-process cocoa powder

1 tablespoon baking powder

1 tablespoon baking soda

2 teaspoons salt

4 eggs

2 cups whole milk

1 cup melted coconut oil

4 teaspoons coconut extract

2 tablespoons vanilla extract

※ Preheat oven to 350°F. Butter and flour four 6-inch, one 8-inch, and one 10-inch round baking pan.

※ In a stand mixer, combine sugar, flour, cocoa powder, baking powder, baking soda, salt, eggs, milk, oil, coconut extract, and vanilla. Beat on medium speed until smooth. Add boiling water and beat again on low speed until blended. Divide among prepared pans.

※ Bake for 35 to 40 minutes, until a toothpick inserted into centers comes out clean. Allow to cool for 10 minutes before removing from pans. Promptly wrap in plastic wrap and place in to fridge to chill.

ALMOND JOY FROSTING

2 cups (4 sticks) unsalted butter,
    softened

8 cups confectioners' sugar

2 teaspoons coconut extract

4 teaspoons vanilla extract

1½ teaspoons salt

2 tablespoons heavy whipping cream

※ In a stand mixer, cream butter until smooth. Slowly add confectioners' sugar, 1 cup at a time, beating until fully incorporated. Mix in coconut extract, vanilla, salt, and cream. Beat on medium-high speed until fluffy.

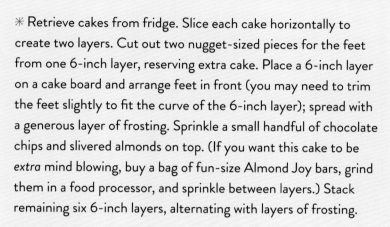

Cake board
1 cup mini chocolate chips
1 cup slivered almonds, salted and
    toasted
1 (5-ounce) bag snack-size Almond Joy
    bars (optional)
Modeling Chocolate, in white
    (page 10)
Modeling Chocolate, in burgundy
Burgundy melting chocolate, melted
½ cup corn syrup
3 cups sweetened shredded coconut

ADDITIONAL
Toothpicks
2 wooden dowels
12-inch thin metal rod

✳ Retrieve cakes from fridge. Slice each cake horizontally to create two layers. Cut out two nugget-sized pieces for the feet from one 6-inch layer, reserving extra cake. Place a 6-inch layer on a cake board and arrange feet in front (you may need to trim the feet slightly to fit the curve of the 6-inch layer); spread with a generous layer of frosting. Sprinkle a small handful of chocolate chips and slivered almonds on top. (If you want this cake to be *extra* mind blowing, buy a bag of fun-size Almond Joy bars, grind them in a food processor, and sprinkle between layers.) Stack remaining six 6-inch layers, alternating with layers of frosting.

✳ Using a serrated blade, create the rounded and slightly tapered shape of the body (see photo page 250). Frost in crumb coat, building up extra frosting for abdomen. Chill until completely set.

✳ Retrieve reserved cake scraps and crumble slightly. Combine with a bit of frosting until a doughy mixture is formed. Sculpt a 2-inch round ball and two arms out of the mixture. Set ball aside to chill. Insert toothpicks halfway into each upper arm joint. Connect to cake with a dollop of frosting, and then frost in crumb coat on the arms. Chill until frosting has completely set.

✳ If you have not added dowels to the cake yet, insert two, widely spaced, into the body, leaving enough exposed to support the head. Stack an 8-inch layer through the dowels, followed by a layer of frosting. Stack a second 8-inch cake, then 10-inch layers, and then final two 8-inch layers, alternating with frosting between each layer.

✳ Once finished stacking cakes, use a serrated blade to carve head into a football shape (see photo page 250). Use remaining frosting to add in crumb coat to head, leaving just a bit aside to later adhere modeling chocolate items. Build up extra frosting, at the front of the head, about ¾-inch thick. Set cake in refrigerator

to chill. Once frosting has set, smooth entire cake with water-moistened fingertips. Chill once more.

＊ Using sculpting tools, carve abdomen, mouth, nose, eyes, eyebrows, and forehead ridges out of frosting. It is essential to keep the frosting cold and firm, so it's best to do this in stages, chilling in between.

＊ Sculpt eyes and claws out of burgundy modeling chocolate, and small spikes out of white modeling chocolate for teeth and eyebrows. Create two pointy ears out of additional white modeling chocolate. Once set, attach eyes, claws, ears, and eyebrows using a bit of leftover frosting. Attach teeth by piping a thin layer of burgundy melting chocolate into mouth area and carefully placing in a bottom and top row.

＊ Bend metal rod into a rough S-shape and insert into top of head. Pipe any remaining frosting to cover rod. Retrieve cake ball from fridge and coat completely in burgundy melting chocolate. Allow chocolate to completely set. Using a sharp blade cut out an oval for the mouth. Coat inside of mouth with a thin layer of melting chocolate and then adhere modeling chocolate tongue and teeth. Once completely set, stick onto top of metal rod.

＊ For the fur, use a pastry brush to apply a thin coat of corn syrup along the back of the head and all over the body (except for the creature's six-pack abs). Then immediately press shredded coconut onto the painted areas until completely covered.

NOTE: When creating a top-heavy sculpture cake like this one, always use wooden dowels as supports and a cake board between every 4 inches to ensure the cake's stability. Hot-gluing the wooden dowels to your base makes things extra secure. To maintain the structure, you'll need to chill the cake at least 30 minutes for every 3 inches you build up, and always keep everything as cold as possible. If you try to assemble this all at once the cake will topple. (I learned this the hard way!)

White Voodoo CAKE

Adam Lambert is easily my favorite contestant ever to sing on the *American Idol* stage. So when a friend of his reached out with a request to make his birthday cake for a voodoo-bayou-themed party inspired by season three of *American Horror Story*, I was thrilled!

The Southern bayou is a dark and damp place, steeped in mystery. With a storied history that's laced with witchcraft, the occult, and voodoo, it's a place best toured with a knowledgeable guide, if you value your safety. This cake is a fun and creepy combination of both the mystery of the South and its deepest and darkest places.

White Voodoo
CAKE

Makes one 4-layer cake

SOUTHERN CHOCOLATE CAKE

Softened unsalted butter for pans

3 cups all-purpose flour, sifted,
plus more for pans

12 ounces bittersweet
chocolate, chopped

2 cups piping-hot, strong coffee

4 large eggs, room temperature

4 cups granulated sugar

1 cup vegetable oil

1 cup sour cream, room temperature

1 tablespoon vanilla extract

1½ teaspoons baking soda

1 teaspoon salt

✳ Preheat oven to 350°F. Butter and flour three 10-inch round cake pans and one 8-inch ovenproof bowl with a rounded bottom. Place chopped chocolate in a separate heatproof bowl. Pour piping hot coffee over chocolate, stirring until completely melted.

✳ In a stand mixer, beat eggs, sugar, oil, sour cream, and vanilla on medium-high speed until creamy and smooth. In a second bowl, whisk together flour, baking soda, and salt. Slowly incorporate chocolate and dry mixtures into batter in stand mixer, alternating in small portions until completely combined (do not overbeat). Divide among prepared baking pans.

✳ Bake for 30 to 35 minutes until a toothpick inserted into centers comes out clean. Remove from oven and allow to cool completely before assembly.

SOUTHERN CHOCOLATE FROSTING

1 cup heavy whipping cream

¼ cup piping-hot, strong coffee

⅓ cup granulated sugar

1 teaspoon salt

1 pound chocolate chips, chopped

½ cup (1 stick) unsalted butter, cut into
small pieces

2 teaspoons vanilla extract

✳ In a heavy saucepan over medium heat, bring cream and coffee just to a boil, stirring constantly. Whisk in sugar and salt until dissolved. Reduce heat to low and mix in chocolate chips. Once chocolate is melted and mixture is completely blended, remove from heat and add butter and vanilla, whisking until creamy and smooth. Allow to cool.

Vanilla Buttercream Frosting
    (page 6)
White fondant
Modeling Chocolate, in red
    (page 10; optional)
Hershey's chocolate syrup
Corn syrup
Red food coloring
2 red birthday candles

✳ Center one cake layer on a serving tray. Spread with a generous layer of frosting, then top with second layer. Alternate between cake and frosting for remaining layers. If necessary, trim edges of top layer to create a perfect dome with even sides. Use remaining chocolate frosting for crumb coat. Chill until frosting has completely set. Frost with a layer of vanilla buttercream and then chill once more until completely set. Smooth frosting with water-moistened fingertips.

✳ Using a small round tip, pipe in decorative details with vanilla buttercream frosting along middle section of cake.

✳ Roll out a portion of white fondant to create the serpent. Sculpt the head, leaving small indentations to insert eyes and tongue. Carefully place on top of cake; if you're worried about transporting the cake, add a small dollop of white buttercream and then place serpent on top.

✳ Using more fondant, shape four crosses and secure to cake using more buttercream (see photo page 252). Paint the middle sections of crosses with fake blood, using equal parts Hershey's syrup, corn syrup, and red food coloring.

✳ For the serpent's tongue, gently heat two red birthday candles over an open flame until soft and pliable (but before completely melted). Mold the ends of each candle together and shape the wick-end of each to resemble a curved *v*. Once completely cooled and hardened, insert into fondant serpent head.

Santa Claws
COOKIES

I've always thought Santa Claus was incredibly creepy. If you've ever given any real thought to it, too, I assume you've come to the same conclusion: He's this judgmental old guy with a ratty beard who breaks into your house in the middle of the night to leave presents and take cookies. That's pretty much the M.O. of most stalkers who sneak into your house and steal your panties, then leave behind a mutilated doll's head.

Okay, I'll admit that comparison is a stretch, but still! Let's look at the facts: He doesn't seem to have any real family or friends. You hear about a Mrs. Claus, but I don't ever recall having seen them together. He's got a fully operational sweatshop. And he seems a little overly interested in children, if you ask me. To say these are red flags is an understatement.

Then there's the name Santa Claus—or is it really Santa *Claws*, which is pretty obviously ominous. Is he a monster? An immortal demon from the abyss sent to punish disobedient children? These ideas inspired me to play devil's advocate and show the not-so-sweet side of the guy who's been stealing Jesus's thunder for years.

Santa Claws
COOKIES

Makes 12 large cookies

SUGAR COOKIES

1½ cups (3 sticks) unsalted butter, softened

2 cups granulated sugar

4 eggs

1 teaspoon vanilla extract

5 cups all-purpose flour, plus more for dusting

2 teaspoons salt

ADDITIONAL
Card stock

Scissors

Aluminum foil

X-Acto knife

※ Preheat oven to 400°F. Draw a hand shape (with wrist) about 3 inches wide and 6 inches long on card stock, then cut it out. Roll aluminum foil into twelve golf ball–size balls, and space them evenly on two rimmed baking sheets. Cover each with a sheet of foil, smoothing it down gently over the balls.

※ In a stand mixer, cream together butter and sugar. Add eggs and vanilla and beat until smooth. Slowly add flour, 1 cup at a time; finishing by adding salt. Beat until fully incorporated. Divide dough into two halves. Wrap one half in plastic wrap and place in fridge.

※ Roll out remaining dough half to about ¼-inch thick on a lightly floured surface. Lay hand template on dough and cut out six shapes, using X-Acto knife or other sharp blade. Repeat with second dough half to make twelve hands.

※ Place palm of each dough cutout over prepared foil balls to give a curve to cookie hands, leaving wrists flat on baking sheet. Important: Flip half of cutouts before placing on cookie sheet to create left and right hands. Bake for 8 to 12 minutes, until tips of fingers begin to brown. Remove from oven and allow to cool completely.

RED COOKIE GLAZE

1 cup confectioners' sugar

2 teaspoons whole milk

2 teaspoons corn syrup

¼ teaspoon almond extract

2 teaspoons red food coloring

※ Whisk together confectioners' sugar, milk, corn syrup, almond extract, and red food coloring in a medium bowl. Whisk until smooth. Add more sugar if mixture becomes too thin or more milk if it becomes too thick.

Modeling Chocolate, in white
  (page 10)
White melting chocolate, melted
Filbert brush
Royal Icing (page 9)
Red food coloring
Card stock
Vanilla Buttercream Frosting, tinted
  green (page 6; optional)

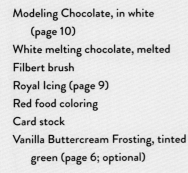

✳ Sculpt claws for each fingertip out of white modeling chocolate. Adhere to tips of cookie fingers using a dab of melted white chocolate.

✳ Once fingertips have fully set, use a filbert brush to paint the wrists of each cookie with red glaze. Tint a little royal icing red with food coloring, and finish by dipping tips of claws into red icing to give a bloody effect.

✳ Using white royal icing, pipe with a decorative tip along the top of the red glaze on wrists to make Santa cuffs. Switch to a small round tip to pipe snowflake embellishments.

✳ For the centerpiece, I wrapped a piece of card stock into a cone shape, secured it with staples, and then crumpled to form a stocking cap. I used my remaining red cookie glaze to coat. Then use leftover royal icing to finish. Arrange cookies around stocking cap on a bed of piped buttercream!

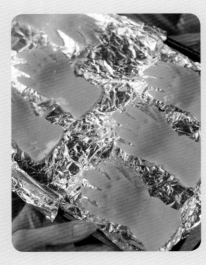

Sugar *Cookie* COTTAGE

Homeownership in today's economy is hard to achieve. Even if you're able to save up enough for a down payment, the amount of paperwork that needs to be filled out could deforest an acre. So what are the alternatives if that raise isn't around the corner and Daddy Warbucks isn't sending any MoneyGrams? I say, build your own home out of sugar!

Around Christmastime, people make a ton of gingerbread houses. Something a little less common and just as fun (if not more so) is a sugar cookie cottage. The components are similar, but the light color opens up a beautiful new palette and the ingredients are so inexpensive, they don't require a credit check.

The fun thing about making an edible house is you can go as far as you like, creatively. If you like balconies, make one of those! Always dreamed of having a tennis court? With a little bit of frosting, it's now within your reach! Personally, I've always dreamed of a snowy little cabin in the woods, which is why I made this.

Sugar Cookie COTTAGE

Makes 1 cottage or about 5 dozen cookies

SUGAR COOKIES

1½ cups (3 sticks) unsalted butter, softened, plus more for pans

5 cups all-purpose flour, plus more for pans

2 cups granulated sugar

4 eggs

1 teaspoon vanilla extract

2 teaspoons salt

ADDITIONAL

Card stock

Ruler

Scissors

X-Acto knife

✳ Measure, draw, and cut out templates for your cottage out of card stock or very thick paper. You will need: four rectangles for the walls (with windows and doors cut out), two rectangles for the roof, and two triangles to fill the space between your walls and the roof. It takes some math and problem solving, so make sure to sketch out an idea of what you want to make and have a ruler handy to ensure your pieces will fit together smoothly. Label each template and mark how many of each shape you will need to cut out. (Note: I left a small opening on the back wall of my house to slide in the electronic tealight candle.)

✳ Preheat oven to 400°F. Butter and flour several rimmed baking sheets. In a stand mixer, cream together butter and sugar. Mix in eggs and vanilla, beating until smooth. Slowly add flour, mixing in 1 cup at a time, finish by adding salt. Beat until fully incorporated. Divide dough into two halves. Wrap one half in plastic wrap and place in fridge.

✳ Roll out remaining dough half to about ¼-inch thick on a lightly floured surface. Lay your templates on dough and cut out shapes using X-Acto knife or other sharp blade. Repeat with second dough half.

✳ Place cookie dough cutouts on prepared baking trays. Bake for 8 to 12 minutes, until the edges just start to brown. Remove from oven and allow to cool completely.

Parchment paper
Royal Icing (page 9)
Blue food coloring
Confectioners' sugar

✳ Cut out small squares of parchment paper for each window, extending about ¼ inch past the edges (these will be inside your cottage, so they don't have to be perfect). Pipe small dabs of royal icing around windows on the backside of cookies, and then secure pieces of parchment.

✳ Place about one-third of the royal icing in a small bowl and tint with blue food coloring. Use white royal icing to glue together all parts of house, holding and allowing to fully set before moving on to the next piece. Once house is fully assembled, decorate the main structure using piped royal icing in long horizontal slats. Use blue icing to pipe a basketweave pattern (see photo page 260) on roof and awnings. Then switch to a decorative tip to pipe trim around windows, doors, and base of house. I also piped in window panes (very carefully) onto the parchment paper windows. Finish by piping icicles with a very fine round tip and then dust the whole house in confectioners' sugar snow.

Peppermint Bark BONSAI

There is something so darn cool about a tree whose leaves have been abducted by the winter weather. There are a million different types, but the kind I mean specifically have those long gnarly branches, knotty bumps, and a twisted trunk. They usually have several roots emerging from the earth, as though they might saunter off at any moment. They are at once creepy and magical.

While they are often portrayed in a dark forest, illuminated by moonlight, I sometimes like to envision them in slightly cheerier settings. Everybody knows and loves the game Candy Land, but what if there really were such a place? I'd like to imagine it filled with delicious trees like this one, with strong bark made of chocolate and the inner pulp made of peppermint. They would be coated in a sweet-smelling snow of candy-cane dust that would fall on your lips as you wandered by.

A life-size place such as this may not exist in this realm, but there's no reason you can't make one in your kitchen, on a *slightly* smaller scale.

Peppermint Bark
BONSAI

Makes one 13-inch tree

3 (12-inch) peppermint poles (you'll only need one, but they break easily, so backups are a good idea)

4 (6-ounce) boxes standard-size red and white candy canes

3 cups dark brown melting chocolate

2 cups white melting chocolate

1 bag round peppermint candies

✳ Preheat oven to 300°F. For the trunk, place a peppermint pole on a parchment-lined baking sheet and place on middle rack of oven. Heat pole about 5 minutes until it becomes slightly pliable. Remove from oven and then twist to break up its rigid shape. Set aside to cool on a parchment-covered cooling rack.

✳ For the branches, heat two candy canes on another parchment-lined tray until just a bit gooey, about 5 minutes. Remove from oven and then pull and twist into odd angles and lengths. Do this until you've gone through two of the boxes and have a wide variety of branches to choose from.

✳ Using either a crème brûlée torch or stove burner, carefully heat the base of peppermint pole and quickly stick it to the surface you will be presenting the final tree on. Then take each branch and heat the widest end until it sizzles. Immediately press into peppermint trunk and repeat until you have a full tree structure. (I used a few smaller pieces at the bottom to give the pole additional support and mimic roots. Don't mind if it doesn't look perfect or if the branches break—some will—because trees aren't perfect and the chocolate bark will correct any mistakes.)

✳ Next, melt dark chocolate and paint all tree limbs, starting at the base, until all peppermint is concealed. (To further support the tree, I also poured melted chocolate into the base of my serving dish.) Pulverize remaining candy canes in a food processor. Melt white chocolate and then pour to create a pool surrounding your tree. Sprinkle with candy cane shards and allow to cool until completely set.

✳ Use remaining white chocolate to delicately adhere round peppermint candies randomly to various branches. Process remaining candy cane shards until there is nothing but dust. Pour into a sifter and gently sift over tree for a delicate and sweet finish.

Predator Valentine COOKIES

Finding romance and hunting for sport have a lot in common: You find out what you want, paint yourself accordingly, and then set out to ensnare your unsuspecting victim. This year I wanted to impress a certain tall, dark, and handsome extraterrestrial, but was having trouble getting the attention I deserved using my usual weapons.

It would be nice if everyone you've ever had a crush on felt the same, but in reality, things can often be one-sided. So what should you do if the object of your desire is disinterested—or, as in my case, from another planet? My recommendation is to bake them cookies! After all, even an alien has to eat.

There's nothing more flattering than anonymously receiving a cookie with your likeness iced on top of it. So do yourself a favor and follow the recipe ahead. I promise your intended will like it so much they'll reconsider that restraining order.

Predator
VALENTINE COOKIES

Makes about 2 dozen cookies, depending on desired size

SUGAR COOKIES

1½ cups (3 sticks) unsalted butter,
    softened, plus more for pans and
    dusting
5 cups all-purpose flour, plus more
    for pans
2 cups granulated sugar
4 eggs
1 teaspoon vanilla extract
2 teaspoons salt

ADDITIONAL
Card stock
Scissors
X-Acto knife

✳ Draw heart shapes on card stock, then cut out.

✳ Preheat oven to 400°F. Butter and flour several rimmed baking
sheets. In a stand mixer, cream together butter and sugar. Add eggs
and vanilla, beating until smooth. Add flour, beating in 1 cup at a time,
and finish by adding salt; beat until fully incorporated. Divide dough
into two halves. Wrap one half in plastic wrap and place in fridge.
(Note: If you're only making a few cookies, the dough can be frozen
and used anytime within a few months.)

✳ Roll out remaining dough half to about ⅛-inch thick on a lightly
floured surface. Lay templates on dough and cut out shapes using
X-Acto knife or other sharp blade. Repeat with second dough half.

✳ Place hearts on prepared baking sheets. Bake for 8 to 12 minutes,
until the edges just start to brown. Remove from oven and allow to cool
completely before assembly.

ROYAL ICING

3 egg whites
1 teaspoon vanilla extract
4 cups confectioners' sugar
Red food coloring
2 tablespoons water
½ teaspoon milk, if needed

✳ In a stand mixer, whip egg whites till frothy. Add vanilla and slowly
add sugar, beating until firm, glossy peaks form. Divide icing equally
between 2 bowls. Seal one with plastic wrap and set aside. Add red food
coloring to other until desired shade of red is reached. Put one-third
of red royal icing in a pastry bag with a medium round tip, and pipe a
line around edges of cookies. Add 2 tablespoons water to remaining red
icing and mix until consistency is similar to maple syrup. Transfer to a
piping bag with a large round tip and fill in the center of your cookies.
(This technique is called piping and flooding.) Allow at least 3 hours to
dry before decorating.

✳ Transfer white icing to a pastry bag and decorate cookies. If the icing is too thick or difficult to pipe, remove from piping bag and add ½ teaspoon milk to thin. (I created this face by piping the general shapes and then using a filbert brush dipped in milk to sculpt and further refine.)

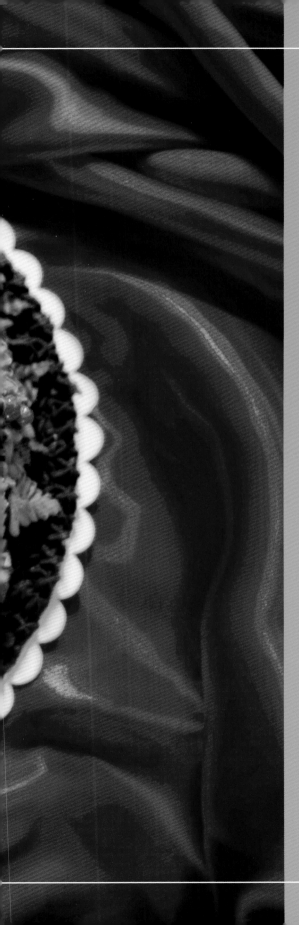

Serpentine Spice CAKE

Life's too short to harbor feuds and blame children for the sins of their fathers; I'm personally a big fan of forgiving and forgetting. For centuries, snakes and humanity have had a shaky relationship, due to one little dispute in a garden several thousand years ago. Well, I say it's high time we bury the hatchet and invite those slithery serpents over for dinner. And to genuinely prove we bear no ill will, I propose that we make it *Christmas* dinner!

I've always loved the glittering lights, delicious smells, and feelings of warmth that are the hallmarks of the Christmas season. One of my favorite holiday treats has always been spice cake, and I've added a secret ingredient to this one to ensure it becomes a favorite of yours as well.

Dense cakes can be tricky. If done incorrectly, they can be dry and unpleasant to swallow. I've found, however, that adding crushed and drained pineapple when mixing a heavy cake is like adding a bit of magic to your baking. What you'll end up with is a cake so moist and delicious, it's capable of mending even the most damaged fences.

Serpentine Spice CAKE

Makes one 10-inch Bundt cake

1 cup (2 sticks) unsalted butter, softened, plus more for pan

3½ cups all-purpose flour, plus more for pan

2 cups granulated sugar

4 eggs

2 teaspoons baking powder

2 teaspoons ground cinnamon

1 teaspoon ground nutmeg

1 teaspoon ground ginger

¾ teaspoon ground cloves

1 teaspoon salt

1½ cups buttermilk

½ cup drained crushed pineapple

1 cup walnuts, salted and toasted

✳ Preheat oven to 350°F. Butter and flour a 10-inch Bundt cake pan. In a stand mixer, cream together butter and sugar, then beat in eggs. In a separate bowl, whisk together flour, baking powder, spices, and salt. Slowly incorporate dry ingredients into wet ingredients in the mixer. Add in buttermilk and pineapple and beat on medium speed until smooth. Stir in walnuts, then pour into prepared pan.

✳ Bake for 25 to 30 minutes, until a toothpick inserted into center comes out clean. Remove from oven and allow to cool for 10 minutes before removing cake from pan. Wrap in plastic wrap and chill until ready to decorate.

FONDANT SNAKE

1 cup light corn syrup

1 cup vegetable shortening

1 teaspoon salt

½ teaspoon clear vanilla extract

1 (2-pound) bag confectioners' sugar

Red food coloring

✳ In a stand mixer, combine corn syrup, shortening, salt, and vanilla and beat until smooth. Slowly add confectioners' sugar and beat until a ball forms. Remove ball from bowl and knead until fondant is smooth. Divide in half and set one half aside. Add red food coloring to other half of fondant and mix well until color is uniform.

✳ Roll out a long rope of white fondant, about 1 inch in diameter. Roll out a rope of red fondant of equal length but about ½ inch in diameter. Coil red fondant rope around white rope in a candy cane pattern and then lightly roll together until smooth.

✳ Use a small piece of white fondant to sculpt serpent's head. Use remaining red fondant to create eyes and additional embellishments for serpent, as well as berries for holly leaves.

Vanilla Buttercream Frosting
(page 6)
Green food coloring

✳ Retrieve cake from fridge and place on a round serving tray. Spread on a crumb coat with buttercream.

✳ Place half of remaining vanilla buttercream in a separate bowl and tint it dark green with food coloring; tint other half light green. To create holly leaves, transfer each buttercream into 2 separate piping bags fitted with leaf tips. Pipe leaves onto individual 2-inch squares of paper with a toothpick inserted in the center (as with Buttercream Roses, page 13). Remove toothpick and place leaves on a cookie sheet. Set in freezer until fully set and ready to apply.

✳ Delicately place holly leaves around entirety of cake, alternating between dark and light green leaves (see photo page 272). Carefully drape fondant snake around cake—instead of wrapping the fondant completely around the cake, separate into separate sections by pinching and tapering ends where needed. Tuck one end under the bottom of the cake on the outside and then tuck the succeeding section under on the inside of the cake. Continue until wrapped from head to tail.

Acknowledgments

First, I would like to thank my family for supporting me in so many ways and giving me encouragement in the early days, when my creations were more dangerous than delicious. Thank you Grant, Dad, SueAnne, and Matt. I love you all so much.

Thank you, Mom, for always being my greatest cheerleader, toughest critic, and best friend.

I can't thank Judith Regan enough for making this book possible. She and her team have been such a blast to work with. Also, a special thanks to Ernest Lupinacci for introducing me to her.

A ton of gratitude goes to anyone who's ever posted a video or blog online explaining their craft and how to do it. The sharing of knowledge is our greatest gift to one another, and I couldn't do what I love if not for your help.

Thank you to Fanny Craddock and Paula Deen for being my greatest culinary inspirations.

To Tim Burton, Vincent Price, Ridley Scott, and Alfred Hitchcock. Your ideas, characters, and stories have shaped how I see the world.

Thank you everyone.

Index